SUPERCARS
OF THE SEVENTIES

SUPERCARS
OF THE SEVENTIES

Jeremy Sinek

Motor

Hamlyn
London·New York·Sydney·Toronto

Published by The Hamlyn Publishing Group Limited
London · New York · Sydney · Toronto
Astronaut House, Feltham, Middlesex, England
Copyright © IPC Specialist & Professional Press Limited 1979

Second impression 1980

ISBN 0 600 38415 2

Filmset in Great Britain by Photocomp Limited, Birmingham
Printed in Hong Kong

Contents

Introduction

In compiling this book, two dilemmas soon had to be resolved. The first was simply that of deciding which cars to include, a task that threw up the need for some sort of definition; what are the criteria that elevate any car – which is, after all, merely an inanimate structure of metal, rubber and plastic – sufficiently above the norm to merit the title of Supercar?

The solution was not long coming, and lies in the two qualities of head-turning looks, and neck-snapping performance. Without these two basic prerequisites no car could possibly qualify.

A Supercar is one with the kind of exclusive and striking (although not necessarily beautiful) appearance which states in no uncertain terms that its owner is as rich as he (or she) is discerning; that unashamedly places style before seating capacity; that causes heads to turn wherever it goes and draws crowds whenever it is parked; and that looks as if it is doing 100 mph even when it is standing still.

Hand in hand with this must be the performance to give substance to the image – performance in the broad sense, to include braking and road-holding as well as speed in a straight line. The kind of performance that is an end in itself and makes external appearances, for the driver, count as nought. The kind of performance most commonly assessed by the two yardsticks of maximum speed and standstill-to-60 mph acceleration times. We determined that to be considered for inclusion in this book a car would have to be capable of accelerating from 0-60 mph in under 8 seconds or capable of a maximum speed in excess of 130 mph, or of course both.

Having quite easily reached that point, the second dilemma lay in deciding which of the qualifying cars would, for reasons of space, have to be left out. That was a thorny question, for whatever the final choice some readers would inevitably disagree with it.

A few 'omissions' were automatic – the cars that to date have evaded the rigours of a

Motor road test. Others were omitted to avoid duplication arising out of their basic similarity to models already included.

The final selection is a wide-ranging one, both chronologically – from the Ferrari Dino of 1971, arguably the first real vindication of the mid-engine concept for road cars, to the Porsche 928 of 1978 (which may be a pointer to the future) – and geographically, with the inclusion of Italian marques like Ferrari, Lamborghini, de Tomaso, and Alfa Romeo, Porsches from Germany and, from Britain, Aston Martin, Lotus, Jaguar and Panther.

The tests are all drawn from reports published in *Motor* through the 1970s. As such, they represent a consensus of the opinions of a team of testers who between them have driven literally hundreds of the world's cars, from the poorest to the very best. And they contain performance figures obtained by drivers with long experience of getting the very best from any car, and accurately measured with sophisticated equipment.

Wherever it was possible without distorting the prose, the tests have been edited and updated, but readers are asked to bear in mind that history has made some statements obsolete; that specifications of the cars featured may have differed from market to market; that some of the cars are no longer in production or have been superseded by revised versions; and that standards by which cars are judged have, in some respects at least, risen appreciably since some of these tests were first published. To minimise any anomalies that may arise out of these factors, however, the tests are arranged in this volume in the chronological order in which they first appeared in *Motor*, and each is followed by a brief epilogue outlining the history of the car since the time of the test.

It is perhaps in the areas of comfort and refinement that cars of this kind have advanced most over the past decade. Advances in those areas that determine a Supercar have not been as great as you might expect. While none could deny that products of the modern school of styling such as the Countach are *striking*, there are many who feel that earlier designs – such as, for instance, the Espada – were more *beautiful*. And the repressive effects of economy and emissions requirements on engine power have ensured that the very fastest cars of today are on the whole no quicker in a straight line than their counterparts of a decade ago. Nor has there been any great leap forward in standards of handling (the *manner* in which a car corners) even if advancing tyre technology has led to measurable gains in ultimate roadholding.

Which way forward is there, then, for the Supercar? Indeed, has it any future at all when pitted against the powerful lobbies of the environmentalists and the conservationists, not to mention the politics of creep-

ing socialism that are in direct confrontation with the very fundament of the Supercar, its high-priced exclusivity? It is a depressing thought that in the long run their future may depend on the whims of politicians.

In the meanwhile, perhaps Porsche's latest Supercar, the 928, is a pointer to the future, with its super-civilised engine that sacrifices the ultimate in performance for the sake of low emissions, long life, reduced maintenance and *relatively* good fuel consumption – relatively, for even though the Porsche (at a shade under $1\frac{1}{2}$ tons) is lighter than many of its ilk, it is still enormously heavy and wasteful of resources in relation to its passenger-carrying capacity. Perhaps, then, it is Lotus who are the trend-setters, achieving light weight through glassfibre construction, which in turn enables them to get still-good performance from an engine half the size of most rivals', with correspondingly good fuel consumption.

Time will tell. But whatever future form they may take, let us hope that there will always be a breed of Supercars which, motoring enthusiasts believe, enrich society – not just those fortunate enough to own them but anybody who can take pleasure in seeing them in the flesh and on paper – just as surely as any statue by Michelangelo or any Stradivarius violin.

JS

FERRARI Dino 246GT

Perfection is an absolute quality found only in nature or that part of it we call genius: it is rarely applicable to the collection of compromises known as the motor car. Occasionally, however, *Motor* has tested cars that closely approach perfection, missing it only in details of execution or performance. Into this rare category comes the mid-engined Ferrari Dino 246GT.

It attained this elevated classification not only because its designers and stylists got virtually all their sums right – it cannot be faulted in any area of importance – but because they endowed it with two additional virtues. The first is beauty – at least in the eyes of everyone at *Motor* who beheld it. The second is the car's forgiving and controllable behaviour when its limit of adhesion is finally exceeded, an important advance for a mid-engined vehicle which revived our wavering faith in the concept for roadgoing cars. But few drivers will ever manage to lose the Dino, for it has the tremendous grip characteristic of this configuration. Unlike some other mid-engined cars, however, it has adequate threequarter rear visibility (excellent everywhere else) and a boot which is as capacious as the airy cockpit. Such spaciousness follows from an overall length almost as great as that of the latest Ford Cortina, yet with an overall height of only 45 in. Pininfarina's graceful styling contrives to make it look a tiny jewel of a car.

Then there is the superb engine, the equally superb gearbox, the exceptionally comfortable ride, the excellent driving position and the well laid out controls. Perhaps the Dino's only significant fault is its fuel consumption, which is rather heavy for its performance; apart from this we had no more than one or two minor complaints about such matters as ventilation and the location of the instruments.

The original transverse-engined Ferrari Dino announced at the 1967 Turin Show was powered by a 2-litre light alloy 65° V6 with four chain-driven overhead camshafts built by Fiat to a Ferrari design for the Dinos of both companies. Two years later this engine was replaced by another of the same configuration but with a cast-iron block and capacity increased to 2·4 litres. For the Ferrari Dino it develops 195 (net) bhp – 15 bhp more than does the Fiat Dino version – at no less than 7600 rpm, and 155·5 lb-ft of torque at 5500 rpm.

Ignoring the choke lever between the seats we found that it always started easily from cold, as is usual with Weber carburettors (of which there are three) by simply depressing the throttle pedal a few times to make the accelerator pumps squirt neat fuel into the cylinders. Once started it idled easily and pulled without hesitation at once. To produce nearly 200 bhp from 2·4 litres the Ferrari engine has to be very highly tuned by production standards, yet it pulls extraordinarily well from low speeds. For demonstration purposes it can be made to do so from 1000 rpm in fifth by carefully feeding in the throttle, although if the pedal is floored at around 1500 rpm the engine will hesitate, maybe die. But from 1800 rpm onwards the engine pulls with real vigour, gathering particular strength at just under 3500 rpm and continuing to deliver a surge of power right up to the 7800 rpm limit – surely the highest of any car currently in series

production. And throughout this rev range the engine is utterly smooth and unfussed, so much so that care must be exercised to prevent over-revving. All this to the accompaniment of a mellow baying from the four exhaust pipes combined with a whine from the camshaft chains and a faint excited gnashing from the valve gear. Everyone liked this exciting noise, but a few of our test staff thought it just a little too loud and found it tiring on long journeys, even though it reduces to a contented burble when cruising at 100-110 mph, at which speed there is very little wind noise provided the doors are properly shut – they need a good slam.

Despite the handicap of considerable weight for a sports car – 23·3 cwt unladen – and by absolute standards relatively modest capacity and power, the Dino is a very quick car. It gets to 60 mph from rest in 7·1 sec , to 100 mph in 17·6 sec, and will comfortably pull maximum revs in top gear giving a maximum speed of 148 mph. The engine is so torquey that this gear often feels lower than it actually is, inducing an initial under-estimation of speed. The Dino's excellent performance in the upper part of the speed range follows largely from its excellent aerodynamics as demonstrated by its flat fuel consumption curve which remains comfortably above 20 mpg at 100 mph. The shape also has other important aerodynamic qualities, for the car feels impressively secure and stable at very high speeds and proved to be virtually impervious to side winds.

Unfortunately the low drag factor does not seem to have counterbalanced the disadvantage of considerable weight – and perhaps of rich-running Weber carburettors – for the fuel consumption is rather poor and once or twice plunged below 15 mpg during particularly fast runs, although the final overall figure was 16·1 mpg on 100 octane fuel. But owners will probably find, as we did, that after the novelty of the Dino's high performance has worn off, it is possible to get along almost as quickly as before with rather less use of the revs and gears; the fuel consumption then improves to the 17-19 mpg level, giving a range from the 15·5 gallon tank of around 260 miles.

Following the Ferrari tradition there is a gate at the base of the Dino's floor-mounted gearlever to define the positions of the five speeds which are arranged Porsche-fashion: first and reverse are to the left of the upper four gears laid out in the usual H. No spring loading is used except for reverse, obtained with a downward push. At a casual glance the presence of the gate might seem to introduce navigational inhibitions, and indeed our testers did need a little practice to get used to the change from first to second. But after a time the presence of the gate is forgotten and the first-second movement becomes as easy and natural – although perhaps a little slower

– as, right from the start, do the movements between all the other gears. The gearbox then reveals itself as being superb with unobtrusive but effective synchromesh which allows lighting changes to be sliced through. The lightness and feeling of precision is remarkable in view of the distant location of the transmission behind and beneath the engine to which it is coupled by three spin gears.

Well-spaced maxima of 41 mph, 59 mph, 81 mph and 110 mph are possible in the four indirect gears. The engine's excellent torque at low revs made it rarely necessary to use bottom gear for anything other than starting off. Only in fourth was some transmission whine audible.

When it comes to getting round corners the Ferrari Dino has all the advantages – and makes use of them. One such is racing-style double-wishbone suspension at both ends. Another is the location of the engine just behind the driver which puts more weight on the rear wheels for good traction in slippery conditions and less on the front wheels to allow the use of fat tyres with direct manual steering. Both these last two ends have in particular been admirably achieved on the Ferrari: it has monster 205 XVR Michelin radial tyres guided at the front by superbly precise, direct steering which gives good feel with little kickback and is one of the joys of the car.

The inevitable result of all this is an ability to go round corners, which makes ordinary cars seem wholly inadequate. Only when trying a normal saloon after the Dino does a driver realize just how effortlessly and quickly he has been going. Terms like understeer and oversteer are generally pretty academic: the car just steers. Further acquaintance reveals that taking a corner under power tends to create not so much gentle oversteer as a useful tightening of the line.

So much for impressions on the road – we needed the relative security of a closed test track to learn more about the Dino's phenomenally high limits. Unlike many mid-engined cars it does not always understeer

with power, and oversteer without it. On fast bends the gentle oversteer tendency was confirmed; on slow bends we were able to make the front end plough outwards with power. Equally, a vicious bootful of throttle in second could break the tail away although in an easily catchable way.

But there is a much more important question to be answered. Even the Dino must run out of grip eventually – what happens when it does? For the practised anticipation and lightning responses of the professional racing driver, mid-engined cars may be fine, but with their centrally located masses they do tend to spin rapidly when all is finally lost, an unsatisfactory characteristic for the more ordinary mortals likely to drive Dinos on the road, one that has made us hesitate to endorse the concept for practical roadgoing sports cars.

Such hesitations are swept aside by the forgiving nature of the Dino. To begin with, helped by a limited-slip differential, it retains a large measure of its traction and cornering power in the wet, although it does have one vice: a tendency to plane outwards at the front on puddles and rivulets perhaps a little more than would a front-engined car. But if you lift your foot sharply off the accelerator in a corner the car responds with nothing more than a slight twitch that calls for little steering correction. Even if this is done when cornering nearly on the limit, the tail breaks away in a gentle and controllable way. It is this safe behaviour in extreme conditions that makes the Dino so outstanding.

To match this handling are brakes of equal calibre. The four huge outboard ventilated discs are operated with servo assistance through a front/rear split hydraulic system. Although the pressures required were rather higher than is usual nowadays – the maximum 1 g deceleration being achieved with a force of 135 lb – the brakes felt immensely progressive and reassuring in their action. As might be expected from their racing heritage, they did not fade either on the road or during our test, nor were they affected by a thorough soaking in the water-

splash. But a really strenuous pull on the handbrake gave a deceleration of no more than 0·31 g.

Few saloon cars other than Citroens – let alone sports cars – ride better than the Dino. Firm, rather than harsh at low speeds, the suspension simply smothers the biggest bumps and soaks up undulations without pitch, float or bottoming. The comfort provided contributes greatly to the feeling of security so characteristic of the car. Unfortunately, the ride is not matched by the seats, which could only suit midgets and have rolls across the tops of their backrests which dug into the shoulder blades of even our shortest drivers. These backrests incorporate adjustable headrests but do not recline – there wouldn't be room for them to do so anyway. In partial compensation for these defects the range of fore-and-aft adjustment is enough to satisfy the legroom requirements of human beings at the other extreme of size as represented by our resident 6 ft 5 in giant. And the seats do provide good lateral support, helped by the rest for the left foot which constitutes an excellent bracing spot.

Sports cars tend to have cramped cockpits; Italian cars to have the steering wheel too far away and the pedals too close. Although the Dino is both sporting and Italian, its small steering wheel (which has a leather-covered rim) and its pedals are so well located that everyone was able to achieve a comfortable driving position, regardless of size. Gearlever and handbrake, too, could be reached without effort by all our test staff when wearing seatbelts. Fingertip control over all the services completes the feeling of unity with the machine that the Dino imparts.

The wiper arms have an overlapping 'clap hands' action which allows them to clear the screen close to both edges, although the wiped area should extend further up the screen for tall drivers.

The deep, wide and steeply raked screen gives excellent forward visibility over the low bonnet. This falls away towards the ground between the wheel arches out of the driver's sight so that there is more car in front than is at first realized, calling for extra care during parking manoeuvres. In contrast the blunt Kamm-type tail is easily seen from the cockpit. It is seen through the rear window which is one of the Dino's most striking features; nearly vertical and no more than 8 in high, it curls backwards through 90 degrees at each end to meet the rear quarterlights set into the flanks of the car. In this way it provides a fair measure of the important three-quarter rear vision so lacking in some mid-engined designs while helping to isolate the occupants from engine noise, and in its protected location at the forward end of the rear deck, remains virtually untouched by dirt or rain. At night the halogen headlamps were good both when dipped and when on main beam so long as their plastic covers were kept clean.

There is virtually no wind noise below 100 mph – it builds up gradually thereafter. Road noise is moderate despite the tautness of the steering and suspension which suggests minimum compliance. Radial tyres notwithstanding, it is more high-frequency roar than low-frequency thump.

Hot and cold air is admitted into the interior through four swivelling 'egg-slicer' vents, two in the footwells and two on the facia, close to the screen but a long way from the occupants. These are controlled by independent distribution levers for each side of the car which flank a central temperature control lever. This is progressive in action but without the two booster fans (one for the footwells and one for the screen) the throughput is small. With the heater shut off, the screen booster provided just enough cool air in town for the warmish days of our test, and the volume can be increased without introducing much extra noise at speed by winding the side windows down a little.

Betraying a desire to match the graceful exterior and the curved plan-form of the windscreen – which is delineated by the deep shelf of the facia – the stylists have given the cowled instrument cluster an elliptical shape. Like the facia it is covered with a black velvety material. Neither the shape nor the material were popular with our staff despite their functional attributes in minimising obstruction to the base of the screen and in eliminating unwanted reflections. Less popular still were the locations of the speedometer and rev counter towards the ends of the major axis of their elliptical enclosure, just where they are dangerously obscured by the wheel rim to all but very short drivers – dangerous because the engine is so smooth and unfussed that even its very high 7800 rpm limit could easily be exceeded. On the other hand at no time did it show the slightest signs of rising temperature or falling oil pressure, yet the relevant

gauges have been given pride of place, right in front of the driver.

Also covered in the velvety material, and retained by a cheap-looking catch but no lock, is the lid of the moderate-sized glove compartment. Together with the boxes built in to the doors this provides most of the oddments space. The front compartment is filled by the spare wheel and toolkit, but the conventional rear boot is large for a sports car, taking 5·6 cu ft of our test suitcases.

The 246GT remained in production for some three years after our mid-1971 road test, the only alteration of note being the offering of a detachable roof Spider version. Production ceased when it was replaced by the 3-litre 2+2 308 GT4, although a truer successor was the 308GTB (see page 104) of September 1975.

GENERAL SPECIFICATION

Engine

Cylinders	6 in vee, mid-mounted
Capacity	2418 cc
Bore/stroke	92·5 × 60 mm
Cooling	water
Block	cast iron
Head	alloy
Valves	dohc per bank
Compression	9:1
Carburettor	3 Weber 40DCNF twin-choke
Bearings	4 main
Max power	195 bhp (net) at 7600 rpm
Max torque	165·5 lb-ft (net) at 5500 rpm

Transmission

Type	5-speed manual
Internal ratios and mph/1000 rpm	
Top	0·857:1/19·0
4th	1·125:1/14·1
3rd	1·524:1/10·4
2nd	2·117:1/7·5
1st	3·075:1/5·2
Rev	2·667:1
Final drive	4·44:1

Body/Chassis

Construction	steel tubular and sheet construction with aluminium body panels

Suspension

Front	independent by wishbones, coil springs, anti-roll bar
Rear	independent by wishbones, coil springs, anti-roll bar

Steering

Type	rack and pinion
Assistance	no

Brakes

Front	10·6 in ventilated discs
Rear	10·6 in ventilated discs
Servo	yes
Circuit	split

Wheels/Tyres

Type	alloy, 6½ × 14 in
Tyres	Michelin 205/70 VR14

Electrical

Battery	12v, 60 a-h
Earth	negative
Generator	alternator
Fuses	12
Headlights	2 halogen

PERFORMANCE DATA

Maximum speeds

	mph	rpm
Top	148	7800
4th	110	7800
3rd	81	7800
2nd	59	7800
1st	41	7800

Acceleration from rest

mph	sec
0-30	2·6
0-40	3·6
0-50	5·5
0-60	7·1
0-70	9·2
0-80	11·4
0-90	14·5
0-100	17·6
0-110	22·0
0-120	28·5
Standing ¼ mile	15·4
Standing km	27·8

Acceleration

mph	top sec	4th sec
20-40	8·4	6·0
30-50	7·8	5·0
40-60	7·8	4·5
50-70	7·2	5·3
60-80	7·3	5·4
70-90	8·2	5·5
80-100	8·9	6·2
90-110	9·5	7·2
100-120	11·8	—

Fuel consumption

Touring*	23·0 mpg
Overall	16·1 mpg
Tank capacity	15·5 gal
Maximum range	356 miles

* Consumption midway between 30 mph and maximum speed less 5% allowance for acceleration.
Maximum range is based on touring consumption.

LAMBORGHINI Jarama

Although at the time of our test in 1971 the Jarama was the youngster of Lamborghini's three-car range (only a few Urracos having been built), its ancestry as the middleweight 2+2 could be traced right back to the 2+1 350GT of 1963, the first car Ferruccio Lamborghini made, then with a 3464 cc V12 engine. That was followed by the bug-eyed 350GT and then the similar 4-litre 400GT 2+2, all with Superleggera Touring coachwork. When Touring folded, Marazzi styled the replacement Islero which was itself superseded by the Jarama at the 1970 Geneva Motor Show.

Although the engine is at the front, not fashionably behind the driver, the Jarama is pure thoroughbred with its double wishbone suspension all round, ventilated disc brakes, four-cam V12 engine, five-speed gearbox, and cast alloy wheels.

The Jarama is not a car that makes friends quickly: it doesn't to our eyes look worth its very high price inside, and one's initial impression is clouded by the poor driving position, heavy steering and indifferently planned cockpit. Soon these things are overshadowed, if never eliminated, by other more agreeable qualities like the superb ride which puts to shame that of many luxury saloons, let alone other sports cars. The roadholding is also outstanding and, on the open road, the handling much better than the heavy steering would suggest when parking. The performance is exciting, the noise exhilarating, the brakes and stability at speed superb. If the excellence of the basic car as an impeccably behaved driving machine were matched in every detail department we might even have tried to justify its price.

As every aficionado well knows, at the heart of this Lamborghini is a magnificent 4-litre 60° V12 engine with two chain-driven overhead camshafts to each bank of cylinders. In the Jarama (and its big sister the Espada) this classic short-stroke engine is rated at 350 bhp at 7500 rpm using six twin-choke 40 DCOE Weber carburettors.

The cold-start mixture control works only on one bank of carburettors (feeding, in effect, a straight-six engine) and did not seem too effective on our car: without a few assisting dabs on the throttle to prime the Webers, the engine was reluctant to start when cold and it usually stalled several times

before you could 'catch' it with the throttle. Once running properly on all 12 cylinders, it pulled without temperament or hesitation even when cold. The pre-engaged starter motor whirrs the engine into action without any of the customary clashing and churning.

When the engine does start you are immediately aware of some very special machinery up front. The mellow hum of six firing strokes to each turn of the crankshaft; the muffled zizz of the cam drive chains; the gentle chatter of 24 poppet valves; the hollow purr from a quartet of exhaust pipes . . . these sounds are orchestrated into a note of memorable quality, one that rises to an exciting – and to some ears an excessively loud – crescendo when the engine is extended. Blip the throttle and the revs leap and fall instantly, revealing not only racing engine response but also a throttle linkage that gives very fine and progressive control over revs and power.

The V12 engine pulls smoothly from absurdly low revs in top gear – 600 rpm when you are showing off, 1000 rpm for more practical work. At low speeds, though, the throttle must be eased in gently (unlike that of the V12 Jaguar which can be floored at almost zero revs) to prevent the engine from hunting and pinking. The camshaft and timing tolerate rather than encourage this sort of treatment, for adequate though the engine is at low revs, it is at high crankshaft speeds that it excels; as the revs rise so the power comes in ever more aggressively.

The acceleration figures show quite clearly how the excess of power over wind resistance in either of the two top gears does not begin to diminish until around 90 mph. With this progressive power surge you are not impressed so much by kick-in-the-back acceleration as a sustained thrust which goes on and on and doesn't begin to tail away until the car has reached 130 mph or so. It was the Jarama's acceleration from speeds at which many other fast cars are beginning to flag that impressed us most.

From rest the acceleration is vivid, make no mistake, but not remarkable by absolute standards: the Aston Martin DBS V8, admittedly with an extra 1·3 litres (but also more weight), gets to 100 mph a couple of seconds quicker, although this slight superiority is of little practical advantage on the road. The rev counter is red lined at 7 200 rpm, which we observed during performance testing for fear that the 7 900 quoted in the handbook was a misprint (they often appear in translated manuals). In fact it was not; such speeds are permissible for short bursts, so our acceleration figures might have been a little better using the higher limit.

With the 4·09:1 axle ratio giving 20·8 mph/1000 rpm (there's an alternative 4·5:1 ratio available) the car will do 53, 77, 109 and 134 mph at 7 900 rpm in the four lower gears: so

even quite quick corners can be taken in second gear. Unfortunately, poor weather and heavy traffic did not allow any maximum speed runs on the return from Italy, and there is nowhere they could be done accurately in Britain. Lamborghini claim 'over 162 mph': after some brave high-speed laps at the Motor Industry Research Association (MIRA) proving ground, we doubt that this particular car would have reached such a speed: something in the upper 150s seemed nearer the mark – as if it mattered.

Needless to say, the Jarama consumes large quantities of fuel (and an appreciable amount of oil in our case, too). Even with a 20·5 gallon fuel tank, the range at a typical consumption of 12 mpg would be no more than a modest 240 miles.

The short wooden-topped lever for the five-speed gearbox (Lamborghini's own) has an Alfa/Maxi gate with fifth to the right of the normal H pattern and reverse opposite fifth. Because the lever is strongly spring loaded in the central 3/4 plane it needs a heavy hand (it would be much easier from the left-hand seat as originally intended) and we were not too impressed with it at first. Familiarity bred a lot more respect, though: the responsive engine and close ratios call for sharp, quick changes which you soon find are easy enough to make provided a firm push/pull is used to overpower some stiffness and the spring loading on the outside gates, and a light one to let the lever self-centre for the middle slots. The change is particularly stiff and heavy after a cold start when the synchromesh on second is easily beaten: once the gearbox is warm the lever moves much more easily and the synchromesh copes well without baulking.

Apart from the position of the pedal, of which more later, the clutch is excellent. Although it is heavy, the effective travel is fairly small – a great asset for quick changes – and engagement absolutely smooth and progressive. The beautifully engineered throttle linkage also assists smooth, feathered changes.

In contrast many drivers, probably most women, would consider the Jarama's unassisted and rather low geared steering intolerably heavy when parking and round-

ing sharp corners. Otherwise it is, if not exactly light, easy enough and a lot more responsive than the ratio (1.25 turns on a 50 ft circle) would suggest. Because the car's handling is virtually neutral, you do not have to wind on much lock to counter understeer, even when the g loads increase to what subjectively feel like very high values indeed.

The car's cornering powers on monster 215-70VR Michelin radials, the 'in' tyre for high speed exotica, are very impressive and it is not so much adhesion that sets the limit as the location of the driver in his seat. On dry roads you can pour on a lot of power in a low gear coming out of corners without the tail even hinting it might break away.

We had no chance to try the car on familiar wet roads in Britain; coming back from Italy in the rain, the car behaved pretty well but tended to run wide at the front on slippery corners, and also to lock the front wheels under braking. Any untoward behaviour like this is immediately detectable through the informative steering, the feel of which is enhanced – at least in the opinion of some drivers – by moderate kickback which faithfully relays what the wheels and suspension are doing. The absence of body roll and tyre squeal are further encouragements to hard cornering.

As on corners, so at speed the Jarama is impressively stable, maintaining an arrow-straight course at its natural cruising gait of 130 mph.

It was from above this speed – and downhill to boot – that we gave the brakes their stiffest test. The four ventilated discs arrested the car all square without judder or fade in what seemed a remarkably short distance. Quite strong servo assistance makes the brakes just a little sensitive and spongy when used gently around town, although much

firmer pressure is needed at speed, and they certainly feel reassuring. The rather feeble handbrake just held the car on a 1-in-4 slope but not on a 1-in-3.

Scepticism born of experience from previous specialist cars led us to expect at best an indifferent ride, so we were surprised and impressed to find that of the Jarama to be remarkably good. The suspension combines those desirable but usually incompatible qualities of resilience for soaking up the bumps, and firmness to minimize wallow and roll. Although the big tyres thump and drum when disturbed, very little jarring reaches the occupants.

Would that the driving position attained the same high standard. The pendant pedals on the test car, although nicely arranged laterally for heel and toeing, were much too close to the seat, the steering too far away – a layout that enforced a knees-up arms-straight position which tall drivers found most awkward, especially as their knees filled the small gap between steering wheel and door/centre console, leaving little room for their hands to turn the wheel. To be fair, shorter drivers did not have so much trouble and one six footer who drove the car for several hundred miles said he got used to it after a bad start.

The seats themselves are not bad. Bolstered edges, assisted by the proximity of the doors and central console, provide reasonable side support when cornering, although it could be even better. Of the remaining major controls, only the gear-lever is well placed – you have to lean forward and down to reach the handbrake. Most of the minor controls are strewn along a ledge in front of the instrument panel, rather like those in Vauxhall's Viva, where they are hardly an object lesson in ergonomics. The only one under fingertip control is a stalk for the indicators, dip and strident air horn.

Individually, the heating and ventilation work quite well, although both have their limitations. The biggest snag – in fact a major fault – is that they cannot be enjoyed together as in many cars costing a tenth as much. The two central eyeball vents provide an excellent volume of air – either heated or at ambient temperature – when the three-speed fan is at maximum speed. But in hot weather and slow moving traffic, the transmission tunnel gets pretty warm and the incoming air tepid. An awkwardly placed water tap beneath the facia provides a measure of progressive temperature control for the heater which, from two swivelling butterfly flaps, warms your feet nicely but makes the air you breathe stuffy.

The best way to ventilate the hot cockpit is to open one of the electrically operated side windows: this means a draught and a lot more wind noise. Normally, the doors and windows are quite well sealed and wind noise thus low, if not as impressively isolated as in the previous two Lamborghinis we have driven – a Miura and an Islero. Even so, the wail of the engine prevents the Jarama from being a quiet car when extended – it becomes a bit tiring when cruising at 120 mph or more – although it is peaceful enough when driven gently on smooth roads. On rough ones, tyre drumming adds to the noise level.

The Jarama is not a four-seater but a tight 2 + 2: even children under 10 found the back seat legroom poor unless the front seats were pushed inconveniently far forwards. Moreover the low cushion and high sill made seeing out difficult for children. Even for the driver, visibility is not especially good. As the corners cannot be seen, it is difficult at first to judge just how very wide the car is. As you look mostly through the bottom of the large steeply raked screen, the parked wipers sometimes obscure vision too, especially on left-hand turns and brows of hills. The wipers can be set to sweep intermittently – useful in drizzle – and a rheostat knob regulates their continuous speed from fast to frenzied.

The four quartz halogen lights are normally partially hidden by eyelids operated through a nicely engineered pillar screw mechanism by an electric motor. A rocker switch on the centre console controls the flaps, which do not have to be raised for flashing as the low-level fog lights are used for this instead. The dipped beam is relatively weak so unless the road is deserted you cannot really go as fast as the powerful main beam permits.

Although the interior is impressively styled – which does not mean that it is particularly well planned – the finish and trim were rather ordinary and not what most people expected to find in this price of car. Perhaps the slightly tired maroon upholstery in the test car exaggerated this impression, for other Jaramas we inspected at the factory, particularly those with tan upholstery, looked more luxurious and better finished.

Behind the line-up of facia switches is a neat cluster of six dials set into an ill-fitting wood veneer board. Your hands on the wheel rim partially mask the outer pair – the rev counter and speedometer – but the others are clearly in view. In the centre is a panel of rather insipid looking tell-tale lights, some of them 'identified' by strange symbols. Small oil pressure and water temperature gauges are also set into their respective gauges. The instrument lights can be rheostatically dimmed.

An armrest is built into each of the heavy doors – these have no stay-open catches and are inclined to slam on your shins. A very hard push was needed to shut the doors properly. Pulling a (lockable) release catch in the driver's door jamb releases the boot

lid. Although very wide, the boot is shallow and narrow, the penalty of having space-consuming double-wishbone rear suspension, a large fuel tank and a monster spare tyre in a short wheelbase car. Luggage accommodation can be usefully increased by lowering the rear seat squabs to form a platform big enough for a couple of fair size suitcases. There is also a handy tray on the central divide by your elbow (partially occupied by the stereo/tape player in the test car) and a deep locker on the facia.

At the time of going to press the future of Lamborghini was uncertain, the company being held in a mild form of receivership following their failure to meet a commitment to build the bodies for BMW's mid-engined M1. After our 1971 test the Jarama gained more power in 1972, an auto option in 1974, and was discontinued in 1978.

GENERAL SPECIFICATION

Engine

Cylinders	12 in vee
Capacity	3 927 cc
Bore/stroke	82 × 62 mm
Cooling	water
Block	alloy
Head	alloy
Valves	dohc per bank
Compression	10·7:1
Carburetter	6 Weber 40DCOE twin-choke
Bearings	7 main
Max power	350 bhp (DIN) at 7 500 rpm
Max torque	289 lb-ft (DIN) at 5 500 rpm

Transmission

Type	5-speed manual
Internal ratios and mph/1000 rpm	
Top	0·815:1/20·8
4th	1·000:1/17·0
3rd	1·225:1/13·8
2nd	1·735:1/9·8
1st	2·520:1/6·7
Rev	2·765:1
Final drive	4·09:1

Body/Chassis

Construction	steel, unitary

Suspension

Front	independent by wishbones, coil springs, anti-roll bar
Rear	independent by wishbones, coil springs, anti-roll bar

Steering

Type	ZF worm and sector
Assistance	no

Brakes

Front	11·8 in ventilated discs
Rear	11·0 in ventilated discs
Servo	yes
Circuit	split

Wheels/Tyres

Type	alloy, 7J × 15 in
Tyres	Michelin 215/70 VR15

Electrical

Battery	12v
Earth	negative
Generator	alternator
Fuses	19
Headlights	4 quartz halogen

PERFORMANCE DATA

Maximum speeds		mph	rpm
Top (see text)	...	162	7800
4th	...	134	7900
3rd	...	109	7900
2nd	...	77	7900
1st	...	53	7900

Acceleration from rest

mph					sec
0-30	...	...	...	...	2·8
0-40				...	3·9
0-50	...			...	5·3
0-60				...	6·8
0-70				...	8·5
0-80				...	11·2
0-90	...			...	13·4
0-100	...			...	16·4
0-110	...			...	20·7
0-120	...				27·0
Standing ¼ mile		...	...		14·9
Standing km	...		...	...	27·0

Acceleration in

			top	4th
mph			sec	sec
10-30	...	...	—	7·9
20-40	...	...	9·1	7·4
30-50	...	...	8·8	6·3
40-60	...	...	8·5	5·8
50-70	...	...	8·0	5·5
60-80	...	...	8·1	5·3
70-90	...	...	9·2	5·7
80-100	...	...	12·6	6·5
90-110	...	...	—	—
100-120	...	...	—	—

Fuel consumption

Touring*	13·2 mpg
Overall	11·7 mpg
Tank capacity	20·5 gal
Maximum range	270 miles

*Consumption midway between 30 mph and maximum speed less 5% allowance for acceleration.
Maximum range is based on touring consumption.

MASERATI Indy

We expected to find strong traces of a competition heritage in the first Maserati to be given a full *Motor* road test because the name of this Italian company is so closely bound up with the history of motor racing. Some traces of this sort are indeed part of the Indy 4·7 – notably its tremendous performance as exemplified by a 0-60 mph acceleration time of 7·5 sec, and a maximum speed of 143 mph. To this can be added the note of restrained ferocity emitted by the exhaust pipes of the engine, an outstandingly smooth and quiet unit, yet a race-bred four-cam V8. There is a racing influence, too, in the taut neutrality of the responsive handling, as well as in the beauty of the body which made the car a crowd-drawer wherever it stopped.

But we found the Indy much more a high-speed inter-city commuter for the wealthy businessman than a car for the driver with sporting tastes, especially in the form tested, with automatic transmission and power steering. And unlike most elegant coupes, for example, this one is a genuine four-seater – albeit with a rather small boot – quite capable of carrying four adults in comfort for long distances. The grand touring role is reinforced by the refinement which springs from low levels of engine, transmission and wind noise.

But road noise is not well suppressed, nor is the ride particularly good. Moreover, in this price range owners have a right to expect something better than the ineffective heating and ventilation and the muddled, amateurish minor controls. A more important criticism concerns the handling, fine on completely clean and dry roads, but in the presence of even a little dampness the car is rather prone to oversteer. We were also rather disappointed in the reliability of our test car, which suffered a number of faults and failures during our brief tenure of it.

Maserati's basic power unit is a four-cam light alloy V8 developed from sports car racing experience in the late 1950s and early 1960s. For the Mexico and Indy it was available in 4·2-litre and 4·7-litre forms, although a still larger 4·9-litre unit could be supplied for the Ghibli. Our test car was fitted with the optional 4·7-litre engine developing 290 (DIN) bhp at 5500 rpm and 289 lb-ft of torque at 3800 rpm.

Like its sister engines it breathes through four twin-choke Weber carburettors and thus was easily started from cold in the way usual for these carburettors by pumping the accelerator a few times to enrich the mixture. After a few splutters it settled down to even running and would pull without hesitation at once although some time elapsed before the working temperature was reached and useful warmth could be obtained from the heater. It is an engine remarkable for its quietness and smoothness, and for the even rhythm of its V8 beat. The exhaust note is superb: not loud but a smooth snarl which effectively drowns what little clatter is made by the particularly quiet valvegear. All these qualities are maintained right up to the 5700 rpm at which the automatic transmission made full-throttle gearchanges.

As the rev counter's red sector starts at 5500 rpm, and as the handbook particularly enjoins owners not to exceed this engine speed for any length of time, we decided we would not bother to squeeze out any more rpm by manually holding the engine in the gears. Not that it would have been really necessary anyway, for in D1 with all three gears of the automatic transmission at its disposal, the engine effortlessly whooshed the car from a standstill to 60 mph in 7·5 sec and to 100 mph in 19·0 sec. And of course with second gear available up to 75 mph the kickdown acceleration was of the 'instant' sort, no 20 mph speed increment taking longer than 6·6 sec up to 100 mph, the mean time being nearer 4 sec. With the 3·31:1 final drive ratio fitted (which is a no-cost option to a 3.54:1 final drive ratio) the car is geared to reach 143 mph in the 1:1 top of its automatic transmission. Unfortunately we were not able to put this to the test, but manual transmission cars with an overdrive fifth gear are reliably known to achieve 155-160 mph, so automatics should comfortably manage their 143 mph, though a truer maximum, keeping to the red-lined 5500 rpm would be 131 mph.

High performance, automatic transmission, an overall weight of nearly 33 cwt and a body designed for looks rather than aerodynamics are factors hardly conducive to fuel economy, although if you can afford the Indy you are not likely to care very much. Our overall fuel consumption was 12·5 mpg, while the touring fuel consumption was little better at 15·1 mpg – derived from a consumption graph that is almost flat from 30 mph to 80 mph. Taking 14 mpg as being what a typical owner might obtain gives a range from the two 11-gallon tanks of just over 300 miles – not a lot for a grand tourer.

Our test car was fitted with the optional Borg-Warner automatic transmission. This excellent three-speed plus torque converter unit has a 'D2' mode (using second and top only), a 'D1' mode (using all three gears) and an 'L' position for second and bottom only, although the transmission will only drop into first if the speed falls to around 20 mph. Its upward changes were extremely smooth, especially on full throttle, as, generally, was the engagement of kickdown. The manual engagement of second by selecting L was also smooth so there was no fear of the back wheels spinning or jerking when using this downward change on entering a corner. The only jerky changes were the kickdown engagement of first at low speeds such as at the exit from a roundabout after being baulked by slower traffic, and when dropping back into D1 on the overrun after using L.

Full throttle changes occured at 5700 rpm, giving maxima of 57 mph and over 92 mph in first and second, a satisfactory spread of ratios giving ample extra acceleration for overtaking. But kickdown only selects first at speeds below about 20 mph, and the initial acceleration when getting second at around 35 mph, say, is less impressive, perhaps because the engine's strength is in power rather than low-speed torque. A little gearbox whine was noticeable at very low and very high speeds, and at very high speeds the back axle also whined a little.

The Indy has double wishbone suspension at the front with coil springs and an anti-roll bar, while at the rear there is a leaf-sprung live axle located only by a single torque reaction rod and restrained by another anti-roll bar. With the help of these two roll bars and a weight distribution not far from the 50/50, this layout has been set up to give an absolute neutrality of handling which will seem strange at first even to experienced drivers. The lack of understeer and minimal roll angles pay off in making the Indy a go-where-you-point-it car with splendidly lurch-free behaviour in fast esses.

Equally, the rear wheels stay glued to the road so long as it is completely clean and dry. The limited slip differential then makes it impossible to provoke more than a faint squeak of protest from the rear tyres during an angled full-throttle take-off, and it is similarly impossible to hang the tail out at higher speeds – on a roundabout, say. And of course the enormous 205 section tyres (Michelin XVRs on our test car) on 7·5 in rims provide more cornering power than most drivers are likely to need on the public roads. Moreover the car is never skittish on bumpy surfaces despite the live rear axle – which does not tramp.

But this reluctance to lose adhesion at the rear on dry roads is exchanged for an almost equal eagerness to do so in the wet or if the surface is to the slightest extent greasy. There is a resultant sharp change to oversteer which calls for very careful throttle control in any but completely dry conditions, especially as, deceptively, the tendency for the back wheels to break traction is more apparent at high speeds than low: again, this perhaps demonstrates a lack of low-speed torque. We therefore feel that this characteristic makes the Indy rather delicately balanced for a road car.

On our test model the trait was accentuated by the dead feel of the optional ZF power steering fitted, a recirculating ball system. It offers noticeable resistance to steering movements at the wheel rim, but it is a resistance that does not rise or fall with increasing or decreasing cornering forces. It requires quite a few turns – 3·8 – for a fairish lock but is reasonably direct around the straight-ahead position, although the car was not always easily aimed on narrow twisting roads with the precision one has a right to expect for the price.

The dual-circuit, servo-assisted, ventilated all-disc braking system copes admirably with this heavy car. The brakes were progressive but perhaps a little heavy, the maximum deceleration of just over 1 g on our Tapley being achieved for a pedal force

leaf-sprung live axle – is designed to give flat, roll-free cornering, the ride of the Indy is not its best point. Although acceptable over-all, it is distinctly knobbly over small-amplitude bumps when the passengers are jolted noticeably. It is however very well damped and controlled over undulations, humpback bridges and the like.

The front seats are comfortable and offer fair lateral support, although their reclining backrests need a bigger lumbar bulge.

There is ample room for a large adult on the passenger's side with another of similar size behind him in the comfortable and well-shaped rear seat. On the driver's side there is only just enough legroom for two such people when the space is suitably appor-tioned between them, while the elegant fastback means bowed heads for those at the rear. The back seat, too, is strictly a two-passenger affair, the transmission tunnel covering being extended over it to form a central division-cum-armrest.

The range of fore and aft adjustment is ample for the tallest drivers when there is no one behind to claim some of the legroom. As the steering wheel is adjustable for rake and reach, and since pedals, gearlever and parking brake release are well located, all our test staff were easily able to make themselves comfortable. But the car is very high-waisted; its flanks bulge; the left-hand wing is a good distance away and the long nose droops out of sight. All these things make for difficult car-park manoeuvring,

of 125 lb. They proved generally immune to fade, however, both during our special test and during fast driving on the road, although they did fade just a little and judder during some fast lapping at MIRA. They were not affected by a thorough soaking in the watersplash.

But they also grabbed, gently but per-sistently, throughout our period of tenure, making the car twitchy on bumpy or greasy surfaces and inhibiting fast driving. Also the foot-operated parking brake proved incap-able of holding the car even on the 1-in-4 slope and gave a derisory and illegal 0 15 g maximum deceleration.

As might be expected when a simple suspension system - incorporating a heavy,

and particular care is needed when there are high kerbs around. Despite the fixed front quarterlights, however, forward visibility is good, for the screen pillars are well placed, while the view through the near-horizontal electrically heated backlight is also surprisingly good. The foldaway headlamps wind up fairly briskly, and once properly raised the beams of the four lamps are superbly effective.

These lights are raised by pressing a switch on the central console, but thereafter are sensibly controlled by a fingertip stalk with side, dip and main beam positions. But the fact that the sidelamps cannot be energized without raising the headlamps and that there are no auxiliary lamps for daytime flashing are just two examples of the numerous anomalies to be found in the muddled layout of the minor controls.

The heater is not very effective, the main trouble being the very poor throughput without the booster fan. It is supposed to be controlled by temperature and volume slides – not working properly on our test car – but distribution is achieved by playing with the curious flick-up rotating screen vents or grovelling under the footwell to find the valves at the ends of the small outlet pipes. Fresh air to the eyeball vents at the ends of the facia is controlled by another lever, but again, very little emerges from them without assistance from the booster fan. Air conditioning was fitted to our test car, and true to form, it is controlled by an entirely different knob in an entirely different place.

Perhaps the Maserati's tautness is achieved at the expense of minimum suspension compliance, for there is much road roar on coarse surfaces and bump-thump on uneven ones – all of which is particularly noticeable at low speeds in town, as the engine and transmission are so quiet. These units retain their quietness right up to around 120 mph when the car loses a good deal of its refinement partly through some gearbox whine and a deeper whine from the rear axle, although few owners are likely to complain about the smooth snarl of the engine at this speed. But the level of wind noise is always low, and the car as a whole is extremely quiet at 100 mph.

Trimmed all in black – save for the roof – the interior of our test car was lavish enough in its equipment and fittings while lacking the imaginative styling and ergonomics that might be expected for a car of this price. In number, at least, the instruments lived up to the price, the main group of three being immediately in front of the driver: a large speedometer and a matching rev-counter with a small oil pressure gauge between them.

Above the central console and angled towards the driver are an ammeter, a clock, a fuel gauge, a water temperature gauge and an oil temperature gauge. The glasses of all instruments cause troublesome reflections.

In front of the passenger there is merely a grab-handle where a glove compartment usually is, but there is a small lockable oddments tray on the console between the seats. The doorpulls form very small compartments of a sort, but in addition each door carries an elasticated pocket and there is another by the passenger's feet. Under the nearly horizontal glass tailgate at the rear the boot is considerably smaller than it looks, taking only 6·6 cu ft of our test suitcases when filled to the top of the rear seat backrests.

The last right-hand drive Indy was built in 1972. In 1974 the two engine options of 4·2 litre (260 bhp) and 4·7 litre (290 bhp) were replaced by a single 4·9 litre (320 bhp) unit. Production ceased in 1974.

GENERAL SPECIFICATION

Engine

Cylinders	8 in vee
Capacity	4 719 cc
Bore/stroke	93·9 × 85 mm
Cooling	water
Block	alloy
Head	alloy
Valves	dohc per bank
Compression	8·5:1
Carburettor	4 Weber 32DCNF twin-choke
Bearings	5 main
Max power	290 bhp (net) at 5 500 rpm
Max torque	289 lb-ft (net) at 3 800 rpm

Transmission

Type	Borg-Warner 3-speed automatic

Internal ratios and mph/1000 rpm

Top	1·00:1/23·8
2nd	1·47:1/16·2
1st	2·40:1/10·0
Rev	1·20:1
Final drive	3·31:1

Body/Chassis

Construction	steel, unitary

Suspension

Front	independent by wishbones, coil springs, anti-roll bar
Rear	live axle on leaf springs, single torque reaction arm, anti-roll bar

Steering

Type	ZF recirculatory ball
Assistance	yes

Brakes

Front	10·75 in ventilated discs
Rear	10·27 in ventilated discs
Servo	yes
Circuit	split

Wheels/Tyres

Type	7½ × 14 in
Tyres	Michelin XVR 205 VR14

Electrical

Battery	12v, 72 a-h
Earth	negative
Generator	alternator
Fuses	12
Headlights	4 Carello

PERFORMANCE DATA

Maximum speeds

	mph	rpm
Top (see text) ...	143	6 000
2nd	97	6 000
1st	60	6 000

Acceleration from rest

mph				sec
0-30 ...				3·1
0-40 ...				4·4
0-50 ...				5·9
0-60 ...				7·5
0-70 ...				9·9
0-80 ...				12·4
0-90 ...				15·2
0-100 ...				19·0
0-110 ...				24·7
0-120...				—
Standing ¼ mile				15·5
Standing km..				27·5

Acceleration in kickdown

mph ...				sec
10-30...				—
20-40...				2·6
30-50...				2·8
40-60...				3·1
50-70...				4·0
60-80...				4·9
70-90...				5·3
80-100.				6·6
90-110.				9·5
100-120 ...				—

Fuel consumption

Touring*	15·1 mpg
Overall	12·5 mpg
Tank capacity	22 gal
Maximum range	332 miles

*Consumption midway between 30 mph and maximum speed less 5% allowance for acceleration. Maximum range is based on touring consumption.

LAMBORGHINI Espada

Nobody could deny (could they?) that the Espada looks magnificent – so strikingly eye-catching that it is almost a hazard to other drivers. Nor is it just a pretty shape. Bertone's low-profile wedge is perfectly acceptable for human habitation and it really does seat four adults: not in Rolls-Royce comfort, but that is not entirely the fault of the body shape.

And then there is the performance, but, fabulous though the four-cam engine is, the adulation we have hitherto bestowed on Latin V12s must now be tempered after further acquaintance with Jaguar's two-cam Anglo-Saxon version which is smoother, quieter and very much more potent in the low and middle speed ranges than anything we have tried from Italy. Even so, the Espada's performance comes in the electrifying class with a top speed that few owners will ever see, and acceleration that keeps your neck muscles in good trim. Provided the roads are smooth and dry (and sometimes even when they are wet) you can make full use of Lamborghini's 350 bhp.

The Espada undoubtedly has looks and performance in a combination that perhaps no other car in the world can match with the same panache. How sad to undermine all those cherished illusions by recording that this remarkable machine is, in the form we tested it (a 1972 registered car incidentally), marred by innumerable detail faults, some of them inexcusable in a car one tenth the price.

The driving position suited nobody here, such is the absurd relationship between seat, pedals and steering wheel: it will need more than the promised adjustable steering wheel to cure this particular malaise. Similarly, the layout of the minor controls (also to be revised) and instruments is badly planned. Refrigeration is part of the standard comprehensive equipment, and no doubt invaluable for cooling the Mediterranean sun: but the heating and ventilation coped badly with the changeable weather of the British Isles.

Then there's the sheer physical effort needed to conduct this 32 cwt machine, notably in parking and steering it round sharp corners. So long as Lamborghini continue to reject power steering as being incompatible with a sporting thoroughbred, others will continue to produce more wieldy cars.

On the right road – fast, smooth and sweeping – at the right time – daylight in good weather – the Espada is an exhilarating machine that is enormously satisfying and rewarding to drive fast: and drive it you must, with a firm hand and a keen spirit. Moreover, as a symbol of success and prestige in the higher echelons of the golden-heeled society, it is surely unsurpassed. But deprived of people to show it off to, or of good conditions in which to exploit its finer qualities, the Espada can be a tiresome, and tiring, machine.

The handbook says pull the choke for a cold start but we were told not to touch it and to prime the Weber carburettors in the usual way, by pumping the throttle a few times. Usually, the engine would catch momentarily and then stop, necessitating a second or third attempt before it would burst into full 12-cylinder song. Once firing properly, the engine would idle – rather fast and unevenly – and pull cleanly straight-away so there was no obvious warm-up period when you had to nurse the revs, although we were asked to wait until the thermometer read 40°F before moving off.

The background zizz and whine of all those chains and valves, the instant response, and the whang-whang noise when the throttle is blipped immediately indicate that this is no ordinary engine. Although tractable enough – the car will trickle along smoothly in a high gear in traffic without fouling its plugs – the engine has little punch at low revs and it does not start to pull with any vigour until 2500 rpm, despite the transmission's relatively low gearing. At around 3500 rpm in the impressive rev range there's the only noticeable rough spot – timing chain thrash, perhaps – but thereafter the revs build up smoothly, easily and noisily to the permitted maximum of 7900 rpm.

The acceleration times clearly reflect that this is an engine that must be revved, not slogged. As you can see from the fourth and fifth gear tables, the car eases away at first: in fact you have to feed the throttle in below 2500 rpm to prevent the engine from going flat and spluttery. In this respect, Lamborghini's four-cam 4-litre V12 engine is markedly inferior to Jaguar's two-cam 5·3-litre power unit.

It is on sheer top-end power that the Lamborghini excels, so you have to use the lower gears to keep the revs up if lesser cars are not to nip by on acceleration.

Through the gears, the Espada manages to do on 4 litres what the (automatic) Jensen SP does on over 7. That the Porsche 911S comfortably beat them both to 100 mph with 2·4 litres underlines what is often said: capacity is a poor guide to performance

The Espada started to feel just a little twitchy at high speed: worse still, there was a disquieting vibration at 100 mph and beyond, possibly created by wind pressure rather than mechanical unbalance. In the words of the only driver who got anywhere near maximum speed: 'The chassis seems to get with it at about 135 mph but the vibration leading up to this is absolutely unacceptable'.

Lamborghini claim 155 mph for the Espada but despite a special trip abroad, we were unfortunately unable to verify it. Our impression is that the test car would probably not have exceeded an honest 150 mph.

Predictably, the fuel consumption is heavy, although the steady-speed consumption curve shows that the Espada is capable of running quite frugally, thanks to its slippery shape and efficient engine. The rather inaccurate fuel gauge and slow fillers meant that the 20-gallon fuel tank (actually two tanks with a small connecting pipe between them) seldom got properly replenished, further reducing an already modest range of barely 200 miles.

The gearchange of Lamborghini's own five-speed gearbox is no featherweight flickswitch (in contrast to the rival Ferrari's which is), but it is a satisfying box to use, provided you are not shy of it. The wooden-topped lever sprouts from a huge leather gaiter, as if to emphasise that you have to strike hard to win. Strong spring-loading in the three/four plane, not to say a long travel and fairly powerful synchromesh that baulks at high speed, calls for firm, sharp movements, particularly when first and second are involved. Only with the higher ratios, and then only when you change up early, can the gearlever be called easy to move.

With a throttle linkage that provides very fine control over engine speed, and a clutch notable for its almost uncanny smoothness (if not for its weight and travel), there is no difficulty in driving the Espada smoothly.

Because the engine is able and willing to rev, the gearing is not all that high for such a fast car. At 21·6 mph/1000 rpm the gearing in top is about the same as that of, say, a Ford Granada. Yet this does not make the car feel fussed or unrelaxed at speed, even though the rev counter might suggest otherwise. Transmission noise was notably absent from the test car.

At times the Espada feels an awkward and ponderous machine. It can hardly be otherwise with such low-geared steering, necessary to counter the effects of heavily laden front wheels shod with monster 205VR15 Pirelli Cinturato tyres. Parking or turning sharp corners is a real effort, calling not only for strong biceps and stomach muscles, but also for vigorous twirling. Hardly effortless motoring. Power assistance, like the excellent Adwest system used by Aston Martin, would, we feel, transform the car.

Despite the gearing, the steering feels much more direct for normal cornering, although acute sensitivity to bumps and camber changes, both of which can twitch

fade – or to any other untoward behaviour for that matter. The handbrake was pretty useless though.

We were less impressed with the Espada's ride than that of the sister Jarama we tested last year. Underlying the car's primary stability in pitch, roll and bounce, there is some noticeable secondary juddering and bump/thump on poor surfaces. However, it was not the ride but the driving position we disliked so much, just as we did in the three previous Lamborghinis. It is the usual trouble: a distant, rather flat-mounted steering wheel badly related to lofty pedals that protrude too far. Get the seat right for one and the other is hopelessly wrong. Inevitably, you have to settle for an uncomfortable compromise with the wheel at arm's length (which accentuates the steering's heaviness) and your legs bent and splayed at the knees. Six people, ranging in height from 5 ft 7 in to 6 ft 5 in drove the car while it was in our tenure and none of them was comfortable.

The nicely shaped seats are in themselves quite comfortable, although the cushions could do with deeper padding, and adjustment for height would be welcome by tall drivers to introduce more thigh support. We would also prefer cloth upholstery to the slippery leather of the test car; not that side support from the bolstered squabs is inadequate. The handbrake, low down on the floor, is also badly placed leaving only the gearlever among the major controls well positioned.

The switchgear seems to have been laid out more for aesthetic effect rather than practical use, the button for the electric washers, for instance, being nowhere near the rocker switch for the wipers – even though there is a vacant space for a combined wash/wipe stalk on the steering column. However, we did like the rheostat control over the wiper speed, and the useful delay setting for fog or drizzle. The wiper

the car off line, suggest some inherent fault in the steering geometry. Road feel, though, is good. You do not have to apply excessive lock to counter understeer because there is not any, the handling being virtually neutral. When exploring the limit, it was invariably the tail that lost adhesion first, breakaway occurring without much provocation in the wet, especially on greasy city streets. On smooth, dry roads, though, the cornering powers are high and the Espada can be hustled through the turns with considerable verve, minimal body roll and unprotesting tyres encouraging spirited cornering. Indifferently surfaced secondary roads could twitch the car off line, and depressions taken at speed graunched the tyres against the wheel arches, sometimes skewing the car momentarily in mid corner.

In contrast to the steering, the ventilated all-disc Girling brakes are almost too light, strong servo assistance making them very sensitive to slight changes of pedal pressure around town. They feel a lot more firm and progressive when applied hard at speed, and they remained impressively immune to

blades are rather short and clear little more than a shallow slot across the steeply raked screen. Even so, forward visibility is not as badly impaired as that to the rear in wet weather, when rain drops settle on the almost horizontal rear window and partially obscure the view. The vertical glass panel in the tail is very useful when reversing but it soon becomes opaque with dirty spray in the wet.

It was the sudden misting up of the front screen, though, that we found so alarming in the test car. Whenever the refrigerator unit was switched off (and you needed it simply to get cool ventilation), humid air condensed on the windows like a wet blanket, completely obscuring vision. Putting the demister on full merely aggravated the problem for a minute or so.

The air conditioning/heater/ventilation set-up looks impressive, with penny-flaps in the front and back footwells, eyeball outlets on the centre console, slots beneath the screen, individual left/right facia slides, and fine adjustment, with rotary knobs, of the fan speed and fridge temperature, both of them monitored by tell-tale lights. But the weakness of the system is betrayed by the under-facia water temperature tap that is either on or off, so there is no proper temperature control which you get with the more widely used air-mix systems. Just as bad, the console outlets are interconnected with the heater so you cannot blow ambient (or super-cooled) air onto your face when the heater is on.

Because there is room to stretch your legs, as well as an adjustable pad to rest your feet on, the front passenger can lounge in real comfort, if not lie back, as the squabs do not fully recline. The back seats – not very easy to reach incidentally – are well shaped and generous in size but legroom is poor and the cushions are practically at floor level so you have to sit with your knees in the air and your thighs poorly supported. Bottom ache soon sets in. Headroom is adequate for all but tall people.

Wind noise is impressively low – as it has been in every Lamborghini we have tried – so the car will cruise at up to 100 mph fairly quietly. Above this speed, the buffeting vibration we mentioned before disturbs the peace; and of course when the engine is extended in the lower gears, you hear all about it.

The Espada is certainly lavishly equipped but the finish and layout inside is disappointing. The head-up instrument panel, for instance, is well stocked with seven clear, neatly calibrated white-on-black dials, but the rev counter and speedometer are badly masked by your hands and the wheel rim.

The leathercloth trim on the doors and centre console was already looking a bit tatty at the edges on our test car and the carpet on

the driver's side, secured by Velcro strips, had come adrift. Stowage space inside is rather meagre – a facia locker and a recess between the seats. The open-plan layout of the Espada does (just) allow access, though, to the rear luggage deck which is generous in area but not in depth. To make full use of it, you need the fitted suitcases offered as an optional extra. The rear window is also a tailgate, released by pulling a lever in the driver's door jamb.

As mentioned on page 17, Lamborghini is being held in a mild form of receivership following their failure to meet the commitment with BMW to build the bodies for the German company's mid-engined M1. The Espada was still listed, little changed since our 1972 test apart from some coachwork modifications in 1972.

GENERAL SPECIFICATION

Engine

Cylinders	12 in vee, front mounted
Capacity	3 929 cc
Bore/stroke	82 × 62 mm
Cooling	water
Block	alloy
Head	alloy
Valves	dohc per bank
Compression	10·7:1
Carburettor	6 Weber 40DCOE twin-choke
Bearings	7 main
Max power	350 bhp (net) at 7 500 rpm
Max torque	290 lb-ft (net) at 5 500 rpm

Transmission

Type	5-speed manual
Internal ratios and mph/1000 rpm	
Top	0·815:1/21·6
4th	1·000:1/17·6
3rd	1·255:1/14·4
2nd	1·735:1/10·1
1st	2·520:1/7·0
Rev	2·765:1
Final drive	4·5:1

Body/Chassis

Construction	all steel integral body/chassis

Suspension

Front	independent by wishbones, coil springs, anti-roll bar
Rear	independent by wishbones, coil springs, anti-roll bar

Steering

Type	worm and sector
Assistance	no

Brakes

Front	11·8 in ventilated discs
Rear	10 in ventilated discs
Servo	yes
Circuit	—

Wheels/Tyres

Type	alloy, 7J × 15 in
Tyres	HS 205VR15

Electrical

Battery	12v, 110 a-h
Earth	negative
Generator	alternator
Fuses	16
Headlights	4 quartz halogen

PERFORMANCE DATA

Maximum speeds	mph	rpm
Top (estimated) ...	150	7 000
4th	132	7 500
3rd	108	7 500
2nd	76	7 500
1st	52	7 500

Acceleration from rest	
mph	sec
0-30	3·2
0-40	4·5
0-50	5·9
0-60	7·8
0-70	9·5
0-80	12·3
0-90	15·1
0-100...	18·1
0-110...	23·0
0-120...	28·9
Standing ¼ mile	15·7
Standing km..	28·2

Acceleration in	top	4th
mph	sec	sec
20-40...	—	9·1
30-50...	10·3	7·2
40-60...	9·1	5·9
50-70...	8·5	6·1
60-80...	9·0	6·6
70-90...	9·8	6·3
80-100.	10·0	6·8
90-110.	10·9	7·8
100-120	—	9·7

Fuel consumption	
Touring*	16·5 mpg
Overall	11·3 mpg
Tank capacity	20·5 gal
Maximum range	338 miles

*Consumption midway between 30 mph and maximum speed less 5% allowance for acceleration.
Maximum range is based on touring consumption.

DE TOMASO Pantera

The de Tomaso Pantera represents further proof – if further proof be needed – that the mid-engine concept works as well for road cars and for drivers of moderate ability as it does in racing. Forgiving on the limit, the Pantera's handling and roadholding far surpasses that not merely of ordinary cars but also of the best conventional sports models. It is matched by head-jerking performance in the same class as the outright leaders of our acceleration league. And because the handling is so safe and balanced this performance (conferred by a 5·8 litre Ford V8 engine) is more usable – in the dry, at least – than in any other powerful car we have so far driven.

But the Pantera is not just a safe and highly accelerative cornering machine. It is completely practical for long-distance touring with a roomy cockpit, plenty of luggage space, an adequate ride and a reasonable level of refinement.

Although our test car, the right-hand drive prototype, suffered a few minor troubles, we were also impressed by the competence of the detail design, and relieved to see little evidence of the amateurishness that so often spoils very expensive cars.

The traditional European condescension towards the big American V8 is wholly inappropriate to the 5763 cc Ford engine which powers the Pantera. In torque and smoothness this beefy unit is equal – if not superior – to most of its thoroughbred rivals, while not lagging too far behind in specific power output. True, it has no overhead camshafts to boast of, the valves being centrally actuated through pushrods, but it does have hydraulic tappets and the automatic clearance adjustment they provide, together with the cheapness and reliability which follow from high volume production. Like most engines of its kind it has a five-bearing crankshaft, and it is strongly oversquare with a bore and stroke of 101·6 × 88·9 mm.

It is the high-performance version of this engine, breathing through a four-barrel Autolite carburettor, that is installed in the Pantera – with minor modifications including the de Tomaso exhaust system which raises maximum power to a claimed 330 (net) bhp at 5400 rpm. Maximum torque is a massive 326 (net) lb-ft at 3600 rpm.

The compression ratio is 11·0:1, a rather antisocial value in these days of justifiable environmental concern, although the engine will run on 98 octane fuel. But mindful of the dangers of high-speed detonation we stuck to the five-star grade for our testing.

Thanks to an excellent automatic choke,

Below, right:
In spite of an electric fan, the Pantera's cooling system could not cope with traffic driving

starting from cold was always prompt and the engine pulled without hestiation at once, eventually settling down to an idling speed of around 500 rpm. In fact the revs usually sounded higher than this, perhaps because of the deep irregular and fairly loud exhaust throb, which at just over 1000 rpm developed into an obtrusive waftly boom that filled the cockpit when driving slowly in traffic. But only under these conditions did we find the exhaust noise unpleasant. At high speeds it settles back to a more moderate burble, quiet enough not to be tiring on long journeys although needing some improvement if only to allow more comfortable radio listening. There were few complaints, though, about the quality of the noise as opposed to its volume: an uneven V8 beat much like the sound made by a powerful motorcycle yet in no way detracting from the essential unfussed smoothness of the engine which is maintained right up to its 6 300 rpm limit.

It was not high revs which fussed this unit, therefore, but traffic, due to the inadequacy of the cooling system, despite the inclusion of an oil cooler. The front-mounted radiator has two electric fans, one controlled by a facia switch, the other thermostatically. But even with the second fan manually engaged, the needle of the temperature gauge moved inexorably upwards toward vapour lock troubles whenever heavy traffic was encountered.

Deceptively, the top-gear acceleration at very low revs does not feel impressive for the size of engine, and indeed is slightly inferior to that of the V12 E-type, a slightly heavier car with an engine of very similar capacity. But the impression is relative, for the Pantera is quicker in this respect than the Aston Martin DBS V8 and its 20-40 mph time is a mere 6·4 sec (against the Jaguar's 6·1 sec). And once the engine gets into its stride at around 1500 rpm it wafts the car forward with imperturbable vigour, showing peaks in its power curve at around 60 mph and again at 90 mph when it begins to leave the V12 behind. All the top gear 20 mph increments from 20 mph to 110 mph lie between 5·6 sec and 6·5 sec; not until the 7·4 sec 100-120 mph increment does a significant reduction in surplus power become apparent. Despite a limited-slip differential, fat tyres and a rearward weight bias, it was easy to spin the driving wheels for many yards on a dry surface when starting off. After just a little of this treatment the clutch began to fade, however, and in any case we found a slightly gentler take-off gave better results for our standing-start acceleration tests in which the car leapt effortlessly forward to 60 mph in 5·8 sec and to 100 mph in 13·4 sec; quicker than the E-type but almost exactly the same as the Aston Martin. Unlike many American V8s, the engine did not seem to lose power at high

rpm. With effortless acceleration like this it is possible to overtake safely in conditions that would be impossible for ordinary cars.

Our test car would comfortably pull the maximum permissible 6 300 rpm in fifth gear, giving a top speed of 137·9 mph. Current cars have a high-ratio gearbox giving 0·705:1 in fifth rather than 0·846:1, and for these cars the theoretical maximum would be nearly 165 mph, but from the feel of the car we would assume 155 mph to be a more likely true figure.

With a touring fuel consumption of 19·7 mph the Pantera's thirst ought, theoretically, to be quite reasonable for a very high performance car. In fact, with moderate driving, a private owner in this speed-limited country should be able to obtain something near this figure, say 17 mpg. But our touring value refers to a computed speed of 83·7 mph, and therefore can take no account of the considerable amount of time that could be spent above this speed, indeed at above 100 mph, nor of the tremendous usage of the electrifying acceleration. So our overall fuel consumption was only 11·3 mpg, one of the lowest we have recorded, giving an effective range from the 17·6-gallon tank of just under 200 miles.

A ZF transaxle – combining gearbox, differential and final drive – bolted to the rear of the engine is the component that makes the mid-engine configuration possible.

Despite the relatively distant gearbox, the action of the shortish gearlever that controls it is light and precise. It moves between positions defined by a chrome-plated gate: there are five forward ratios, first being away from the driver and back – opposite reverse – while the remaining four are arranged in the usual H-pattern.

Some of our drivers complained of difficulty in steering the lever into the appropriate slots, but these difficulties faded away after a little practice, those who drove this car the longest praising the gearbox for the very quick changes possible with it. The synchromesh on fourth was just a trifle weak, however, while third was slightly baulky and reverse slightly more so. There was some whine in fourth, and also in fifth, especially at just under 80 mph.

This excellent gearbox – overall we rated it nearly as highly as the Ferrari Dino's – was associated with a rather sticky throttle linkage and mated to a progressive but exceedingly heavy clutch requiring no less than 70 lb to depress it – almost certainly the highest force we have recorded.

Even by the standards of the very best conventional sports cars it is easy to be surprised by the speeds at which it is possible. to take corners in a good mid-engined machine like the Pantera which has double wishbone suspension at both ends. These cornering speeds follow as much from the immediate response and lack of roll as from the cornering power – although this is so high that it is seldom exceeded on public roads in the dry. If it is, the handling proves to be quite forgiving: front-end breakaway can be felt through the steering; rear-end breakaway is progressive and controllable. This general praise needs considerable qualification, but unfortunately our further and more detailed impressions are complicated by the fact that it became necessary to change the front tyres towards the end of the test.

When the car first arrived it understeered strongly under power, particularly in the wet when the front wheels tended to plough off quite easily. Under these conditions we also found it necessary to exercise care when using the throttle as the car snakes on greasy patches, despite the limited slip differential. Even so, the general feedback to the driver was so good that it was still possible to drive quickly in the wet, and short of additional complications such as four-wheel drive there is no way in which such a powerful car can be made foolproof against insensitive jabbing of the throttle. But we felt less tolerant of the understeer.

Then bad wear of the front tyre inner edges was noticed, and this was soon diagnosed as being due to excessive toe-out – which causes understeer. The geometry was correct, but at short notice it was not possible to obtain a pair of new Michelin 185/70 XVRs

to replace the worn front covers, and instead larger 195-section tyres were fitted, leaving the 215-section rear tyres unchanged.

With these slightly fatter than standard tyres, the handling was considerably improved. As for most mid-engined cars the basic characteristic was understeer under power, with mild tuck-in or oversteer when cornering on a trailing throttle. But there is so much power that it was possible to hang the tail out on the slower corners. But we would still prefer a little less understeer and suggest that 215-section tyres be fitted at the front as well as at the rear as is standard practice for the GTS model. At all times, however, the car was completely stable at high speeds.

A constant factor in this – and a constant disappointment – was the rack and pinion steering. Here de Tomaso have failed to exploit one of the mid-engine configuration's most important advantages: the ability to allow light, precise steering while running on very fat front tyres. The Pantera's steering is heavy for parking manoeuvres – although lighter at high speeds – and low-geared, requiring 1.1 turns to follow a 50 ft circle. It also has a poor lock. Moreover, it is frictionally stiff and rather dead around the straight-ahead position with little self-centring action. There is not much kickback, however, and on lock the feel of the road is good.

Big ventilated disc brakes are fitted to all four corners of the car with servo assistance and a tandem master cylinder. They clawed the car down from high speeds in a very satisfactory and reassuring manner except that the pedal travel was rather long. A smell of hot linings was observed at times during our fade test, and at around the 8th stop the pedal pressure rose by 10 lb – enough to be subjectively noticeable – but subsequently recovered and remained unchanged for the rest of the test.

At low speeds the motion of the Pantera is rather harsh and choppy and on certain surfaces there is an uncomfortable high-frequency bounce oscillation. There is the occasional trace of pitch on undulations, but the suspension is well damped and at high speeds the ride smooths out to become very comfortable. The seats are rather hard with fair lateral support but not much lumbar support; there is just enough space between their backrests and the rear bulkhead to allow limited use of the reclining mechanism provided. The range of fore-and-aft adjustment was adequate for the tallest drivers, but several members of our test staff disliked the location of the pedals which are strongly offset to the left to clear the right-hand wheel arch.

Three levers at the top of the central console are supposed to control the decidedly poor heating and ventilation system, but even at well over 100 mph the air input from ram effect alone was negligible. The flow through the screen and footwell vents remains poor when the two-speed booster fan is at full blast, and with the maximum temperature selected we were able to get no better than a barely discernible trickle of warmth. Fortunately a greater volume is admitted by the facia vents which also deliver the cooled air provided by the optional air conditioning system which helped a lot to make the car comfortable during warm weather.

Forward visibility is good although the wiper blades leave the upper part of the screen unswept. Visibility directly to the rear is also good, but three-quarter rear visibility is poor. The 7 in circular pop-up headlamps gave a good blaze of light, and for daylight flashing there are a pair of fixed auxiliary lights.

As already implied it is usually the engine that makes the predominant noise, but road noise – when audible – was moderate. Wind noise on our test car was very low up to 120 mph when the driver's window began to flutter due to a slightly damaged door seal.

Insufficient luggage space is often a weakness of mid-engined cars, but the Pantera scores well in this respect with a capacious luggage tray under the long, hinged rear deck. It took a very reasonable 4·8 cu ft of our test suitcases, but it is not the place for perishables like butter, as engine heat makes it rather warm. Poor accommodation for oddments is another defect of the breed, and in this the Pantera gets fair marks; there is a small box on the transmission tunnel plus a small lockable glove box and pockets in the doors.

The general standard of finish, inside and out, and the layout of the instruments and minor controls was much better than is usual for expensive cars of this sort, although few of our test staff liked the black velvety material used to cover the facia.

A large, attractively styled rev-counter and a matching speedometer are mounted directly in front of the driver where they are easy to see. But their glasses are parallel to their nearly vertical faces and often created unwanted reflections. The remaining instruments are located in the central console: an ammeter, fuel gauge, water temperature gauge and oil pressure gauge.

Little has changed with the Pantera since *Motor*'s test in mid-1972. Modifications to comply with noise and emmissions regulations have only slightly blunted the edge of the 5·8-litre V8's output – now quoted at 310 bhp (DIN) for the GTS – while under-the-skin changes include a wider cockpit and adjustable pedals to improve accommodation and driving position. A rear spoiler is fitted to improve the flow of air into the engine compartment.

GENERAL SPECIFICATION

Engine

Cylinders	8 in vee
Capacity	5763 cc
Bore/stroke	101·6 × 88·9 mm
Cooling	water
Block	cast iron
Head	cast iron
Valves	ohv pushrod
Compression	11:1
Carburettor	Autolite 4-barrel downdraught
Bearings	5 main
Max power	330 bhp (net) at 5400 rpm
Max torque	325 lb-ft (net) at 3600 rpm

Transmission

Type	ZF 5-speed manual (transaxle)

Internal ratios and mph/1000 rpm

Top	0·85:1/21·9
4th	0·96:1/19·3
3rd	1·09:1/17·0
2nd	1·47:1/12·6
1st	2·42:1/7·7
Rev	2·87:1
Final drive	4·22:1

Body/Chassis

Construction	unitary, all steel

Suspension

Front	independent by double wishbones, coil springs, anti-roll bar
Rear	independent by double wishbones, coil springs, anti-roll bar

Steering

Type	rack and pinion
Assistance	no

Brakes

Front	11·1 in ventilated discs
Rear	11·7 in ventilated discs
Servo	yes
Circuit	dual

Wheels/Tyres

Type	7 × 15 in (front); 8 × 15 in (rear)
Tyres	185/70 VR15 (front); 215/70 VR15 (rear)

Electrical

Battery	12v, 72 a-h
Earth	negative
Generator	alternator
Fuses	14
Headlights	7 in retractable

PERFORMANCE DATA

Maximum speeds

	mph	rpm
Top	137·9	6300
4th	122	6300
3rd	107	6300
2nd	80	6300
1st	48	6300

Acceleration from rest

mph	sec
0-30	2·3
0-40	3·0
0-50	4·3
0-60	5·8
0-70	7·2
0-80	9·1
0-90	11·1
0-100	13·4
0-110	16·7
0-120	20·8
Standing ¼ mile	14·0
Standing km	25·5

Acceleration in

mph	top sec	4th sec
20-40	6·4	4·9
30-50	6·5	5·0
40-60	6·3	4·7
50-70	5·6	4·4
60-80	5·9	4·3
70-90	5·9	4·5
80-100	5·7	4·8
90-110	6·5	5·6
100-120	7·4	7·2

Fuel consumption

Touring*	19·7 mpg
Overall	11·3 mpg
Tank capacity	17·6 gal
Max range	347 miles

*Consumption midway between 30 mph and maximum speed, less 5% allowance for acceleration.
Maximum range is based on touring consumption.

ALFA ROMEO Montreal

It was in mid-1972 that the first right-hand drive Alfa Romeo Montreals began to arrive in the UK – almost five years after the Bertone dream car was first displayed in Canada and a year after it went on sale in Italy. The Montreal endured, to put it mildly, a slow and painful birth. First, the dream car of the Montreal show was little more than a one-off exotic shape fitted with a 1600 cc engine which made it mobile: to turn the fantasy into fact, a great deal of design and development work was necessary on the power unit – a detuned version of the V8 Alfa '33' racing engine, in light alloy with four overhead camshafts and many other sophisticated features. Then, as the car neared the production stage, strikes in the Bertone factory

set it back several months. But Alfa Romeo managed to get 700 built during 1971, nearly all of which were sold in Italy, and a right-hand drive car was shown at Earls Court in October 1971.

Surprisingly in such an upmarket sports car, the Montreal's layout is conventional; the front mounted engine drives through a five-speed gearbox to a live rear axle. Whether or not it was originally conceived as an advanced car cannot be asserted with any certainty, but several points in addition to its outward appearance suggest that it may have been intended as a mid-engined machine. The two rear seats are so unusable that four adults could not travel in the car at all – and it is more comfortable to seat three in front than condemn one to the rear; this and the tiny luggage compartment suggest a hastily re-conceived design.

But whatever its background, the production Montreal has had to stand and be evaluated against the stern competition of other high priced sporting machinery. In some ways it comes out very well; the engine and gearbox are delightful, earning enthusiastic praise from our testers. The basic structure of the car seems sound, and lacking in noise, harshness or vibration. Yet several points of detail design, such as the ventilation, and the pedal layout, let it down badly. And although the car attracted many admirers during the test, we felt the very concept of an expensive yet traditional two-seater sports car with almost no luggage space would weigh heavily against its chances of success.

One of the best features of the Montreal is its exceptionally smooth 2 593 cc engine. Based on the '33' racing engine, this over-square 90 degree V8 produces 200 bhp (DIN) at its indicated maximum of 6 500 rpm. Maximum torque occurs at 4 750 rpm, which seems quite high until you see that at least 90 per cent of its torque of 173·5 lb-ft (DIN) is available between 3 000 and 6 000 rpm. Other standard features of this impressive power unit are dry sump lubrication, electronic ignition, four overhead camshafts, and fuel injection. Plenty of aluminium and magnesium alloys are used throughout its construction to keep weight to a minimum.

Unusually for an Alfa it is important not to touch the throttle before starting the engine, whether it is hot or cold. After a cold start, a couple of minutes should be spent warming the engine up, after which it will pull quite cleanly and smoothly although full throttle should not be used until the water temperature has reached its normal working level. Driving slowly around town the exceptional flexibility of the engine is very welcome, if marred by a pronounced exhaust boom at about 1 500 rpm; it's surprising just how often such low revs are in use.

Given the opportunity to use the full performance available, the engine runs up to its rev limit with delightful ease. Beautifully balanced, there is not a hint of unwanted vibration, fussiness or unpleasant mechanical noise. It is just capable of reaching full revs in fifth gear, although even with prolonged flat-out running it did not tend to over-rev itself in either direction on our maximum speed runs. The average came out at 135·2 mph, almost identical to Alfa's claimed 136 mph. After three or four miles of running at over 125 mph the oil temperature gauge starts to climb quite rapidly, but it drops back just as quickly if you ease off to cruise at about 120 mph. Apart from this, the low speed boom, and the occasional subdued popping noises from the exhaust on the

overrun, we have no complaints about this engine. At the other end of the range we were able to pull away in fourth gear from 10 mph and from just below 20 mph in fifth without any chugging sensation: the acceleration figures in each gear are a testimony to the flexibility of the car. From a standing start we might have hoped for slightly more dramatic figures, for the Montreal would be blown off quite easily by several sports cars of similar price. By any other standard, of course, 0-70 mph in 10·4 sec is quite fast, to say the least.

In terms of economy it does not seem to make too much difference how hard the car is driven. Gentle driving never rewarded us with more than 14·9 mpg, while on one long high speed trip it only fell to 13·1 mpg. The 14-gallon fuel tank gives the car a meagre range of about 200 miles.

The Montreal's gearbox is one of the few major components of the car not made by Alfa Romeo: produced by ZF, it is a superb five-speed, all synchromesh unit giving well selected speeds of 39 mph, 58 mph, 92 mph and 120 mph in the intermediate gears. Despite being quite high, first gear took a 1-in-3 hill start in its stride. Even from a cold start there is no baulking feel to the gearchange and the short lever can be moved around very quickly without fear of error. The feeling of quality in the gearchange derives from the silence of the transmission and impression of precision and strength that it conveys to the driver. The lever tends to return to the central 2-3 plane under spring pressure, and although first gear is not in the same plane as second none of our team, once they had discovered the correct technique (no force), found this awkward in congested traffic where frequent movement between first and second is required. In selecting reverse we sometimes had to de-clutch a second time before succeeding. According to our figures the clutch, like those of most powerful cars, is rather heavier than average, but although a 40 lb pressure was needed to operate it we were not aware of any conscious effort here. Clutch travel is reasonably short. A limited slip differential is fitted as standard to the Montreal.

The front-engined, live rear axle layout of the Montreal may seem a little unpromising in terms of roadholding and handling when compared with more advanced high-priced sports cars. While there certainly are cars that will get round a given corner more quickly, the roadholding is sufficiently above average to avoid any criticism from us. But while the Montreal is a car that inspires confidence for hard driving on dry roads we found the suspension a bit soft when pushed to the limit. For a sports car, there is considerable body roll on corners and the nose dips quite sharply under heavy braking, all of which detracts somewhat from the pleasure of driving it hard along twisting roads. There could be more feel in the steering too, which is of the recirculating ball type. The car is very stable in a straight line even when running near its maximum speed in cross winds.

On dry roads the Montreal tends to under-steer slightly at first, this being followed by a gentle transition into neutral or oversteer. The lack of strong understeer veils the fact that the steering is quite low-geared – despite the big Michelin tyres it is not over-heavy to park. There is sufficient power available to make the limited slip differential essential for fast driving for it is possible to chuck the tail out and get both wheels spinning even in third gear on some surfaces. Like many high powered cars fitted

with live axles, torque reaction in the trans-mission under full power makes it oversteer more on right-handers than left-hand bends. The smooth torque of the engine helps make power oversteer controllable, and if you feel really enthusiastic, seemingly impossible amounts of opposite lock can be applied without much fear of losing it. If a rear wheel gets caught in a pothole or sunken drain cover while cornering, the tail usually hops a bit but not enough to cause any alarm.

On wet roads the roadholding is still quite good although very sensitive throttle control is required for high speed driving. The kind of carefree use of the throttle that is per-missible on dry roads will end in a spin (which did not happen to us, in case you were wondering!). Once the rear wheels start to spin in the wet, lateral adhesion is lost very quickly, requiring an instantaneous and accurate application of opposite lock. If you have the ability to experiment, however, it is not hard to know just how much power may be used in the wet, and the limited slip differential enables almost full acceleration to be used in a straight line on slippery surfaces. The tail can be felt swaying gently as the car rockets up the road.

Less reassuring are the brakes, which seem to be over-cooled. In our tests at MIRA, we found that a 1 g stop was impossible with cold brakes however hard we pressed the pedal. After the fade test, which the Montreal's brakes passed without so much as smelling hot or juddering, we tried some more panic braking and found that a 1 g stop could be achieved with a pedal pressure of 100 lb. On the road too, the brakes begin to feel better after repeated punishment, which is not always possible or desirable: without this treatment the big ventilated discs seem to stay well below their optimum working temperature. While they may feel rather uncertain and a bit spongy, the brakes should never let you down in an emergency: high temperature boiling point fluid is used in the dual circuits and there is a brake ratio balancing device to prevent the rear wheels locking up before the fronts. Although the handbrake needed a good tug, it held the car in both directions on the 1-in-3 hill without difficulty. The brakes were unaffected by the waterplash.

You can tell straight away, even when trundling around city streets, that the Montreal has a live rear axle. Although the ride is pretty soft, the back end reacts to poor roads with little twitches which betray its suspension system but cause no discomfort. In fact, the Montreal is a most comfortable car; and the brushed nylon upholstered front seats provide support in the right places. The arrangement in the back, however, is not so praiseworthy, for although the car looks like a two plus two, there is no way that three, let alone four, people can be comfort-

able even on short journeys.

The driving position is quite good even though it suffers slightly from the 'built for Italian midgets' syndrome: even our tallest drivers found it reasonably comfortable. Less acceptable is the pedal layout although to be fair the Montreal is no worse in this respect than many other expensive cars. But this is no excuse for pedals that are too far from the floor even for drivers with large size shoes, nor for a brake/throttle pedal relationship that made heel and toe gear-changes almost impossible.

To the left of the clutch, and placed high enough to prevent accidental operation, is a button for the electric wash/wipe system. Rocker switch controls for the two-speed wipers, electric windows (optional), interior lighting, and horn are located in the central console. There is a push button for the horns in each spoke of the steering wheel: the rocker switch is used to select air horns or a quieter tone for city traffic.

The indicator and light stalks are on the steering column. The former feels horribly vague and tends to self-cancel prematurely. The lighting stalk is much better: one twist for sidelights also operates the servo system for the stone guards (are they really useful or just a gimmick?), a further twist turns on the excellent headlights. Forward visibility is good, even in rain, for the wipers are very efficient, and with three rear view mirrors (one on each door, one inside) overtaking should be a safe manoeuvre every time. Rear three-quarter vision, however, is dreadful and can require awkward neck-craning at angled T-junctions.

Apart from the boom at 1500 rpm, which is very severe, the Montreal is a quiet car suffering little from wind or road noise and not at all from transmission noise. Those who put comfort and silence first in a list of priorities will find the Montreal more than satisfactory, provided they opt for air conditioning. Our car was fitted with ordinary fresh air heating and ventilation and in this respect was worse than many cheap saloons. The outlets were badly placed and there was no means of getting hot air to the floor with cold air above: the floor outlets could be closed, but otherwise it was either hot up and down or cold up and down.

The Montreal is fitted with a bizarre set of instruments, so designed that we all found them very hard, if not impossible, to take in at a glance. This is odd since Alfa Romeo usually excel in this department. Instrumentation is most comprehensive, however, and includes a large number of useful warning lights.

The interior trim and furniture is of very high quality but, to some people, shares with the exterior of the car a tendency to be over-ornate. There is not much stowage space, even in the boot, although a large suitcase could be placed on the rear seats if necessary. In the front there is a small ledge in front of the passenger with a cigarette packet-sized ledge in front of the driver (forming part of the hinged cover for the smartly labelled fuse box). Access to the rear compartment is via the rear window, which has a lockable release catch in the driver's doorway. The tiny boot is concealed under a hinged flap: the spare wheel, jack and toolkit are located beneath the floor of the boot.

The Alfa Romeo Montreal was introduced at the Geneva Motor Show in 1970 as the realization of an earlier design study. The car was manufactured under contract by Bertone, and remained essentially unchanged throughout its production run. The Montreal was discontinued in 1975 after the contracted 10 000 cars had been completed.

GENERAL SPECIFICATION

Engine

Cylinders	8 in vee
Capacity	2 593 cc
Bore/stroke	80 × 64·5 mm
Cooling	water
Block	alloy
Head	alloy
Valves	dohc per bank
Compression	9:1
Fuel injection	Alfa Romeo-Spica indirect
Bearings	5 main
Max power	200 bhp (DIN) at 6 500 rpm
Max torque	173·5 lb-ft (DIN) at 4 750 rpm

Transmission

Type	ZF 5-speed manual
Internal ratios and mph/1000 rpm	
Top	0·79:1/21·0
4th	1·00:1/18·4
3rd	1·35:1/14·1
2nd	1·99:1/9·0:1
1st	3·30:1/6·1
Rev	3·01:1
Final drive	4·01:1

Body/Chassis

Construction	all-steel monocoque

Suspension

Front	independent with wishbones, coil springs, anti-roll bar
Rear	live axle with two trailing arms, A-bracket, coil springs

Steering

Type	recirculating ball
Assistance	no

Brakes

Front	10·75 in ventilated discs
Rear	11·25 in ventilated discs
Servo	yes
Circuit	split

Wheels/Tyres

Type	alloy, 6½J × 14 in
Tyres	Michelin XVR 195/70 VR14

Electrical

Battery	12v, 64 a-h
Earth	negative
Generator	alternator
Fuses	16
Headlights	4 round

PERFORMANCE DATA

Maximum speeds

	mph	rpm
Top	135·2	6 440
4th	120	6 500
3rd	92	6 500
2nd	59	6 500
1st	39	6 500

Acceleration from rest

mph	sec
0-30	3·0
0-40	4·3
0-50	6·3
0-60	8·1
0-70	10·4
0-80	13·4
0-90	16·6
0-100...	21·7
0-110...	27·8
Standing ¼ mile	15·7
Standing km..	28·4

Acceleration in

mph	top sec	4th sec
10-30	—	7·7
20-40	9·0	7·6
30-50	8·8	6·9
40-60	8·0	6·1
50-70	8·1	6·1
60-80	8·3	6·1
70-90	8·8	6·8
80-100	9·7	7·7
90-110	10·9	9·1

Fuel consumption

Touring (estimated)*	14·9 mpg
Overall	13·8 mpg
Tank capacity	14 gal
Max range	208 miles

*Consumption midway between 30 mph and maximum speed less 5% allowance for acceleration.
Maximum range is based on touring consumption.

LOTUS Europa Special

Introduced in 1967, the Lotus Europa can take the credit for being one of the first cars to bring the amidships engine layout within reach of the less wealthy sports car enthusiast – the only previous mid-engined production cars being the Matra Djet, the much more expensive Lamborghini Miura and Ferrari Dino. But unfortunately Lotus designed a number of defects into the first Europa, including limited space for your feet and (typical of mid-engined cars) very poor rear three-quarter visibility. And there were a few more faults besides: modest performance, a poor gearchange from the Renault-based drive-train, and a jolty ride over poor surfaces.

Many of these faults were rectified with the introduction of the Europa Twin-Cam, endowed with performance much closer to that of its more conventional stablemate, the Elan. However, no suitable alternative to the Renault 16 gearbox could be found, and because of its modest torque capacity the more powerful Big Valve engine as used in the Elan Sprint was not available as an option. By lowering the floor pan and revising the seats, interior accommodation was much improved (although foot space was still limited) and the rear three-quarter visibility was made better – although only from dismal to mediocre – by cutting away the fins behind the passenger compartment. The gearchange, too, was still not acceptable for a

With a four-cylinder engine, the Europa has acceleration in the Supercar class

sports car even though the linkage was modified.

Mechanically, the Special is identical to the Twin-Cam except for two important changes; it has the Big Valve engine, and there is an alternative five-speed gearbox, Lotus having had time to find that there is enough strength in the four speeder to offer both. The model tested here has the five speed box which is basically as fitted to the Renault 16TS but with Lotus' own fifth gear; it also sports a much improved linkage.

These changes made the Europa into a very good car. The handling and road-holding are probably as close to racing standards as is possible to get anywhere in the world without buying a track car, while the ride must be the envy of many a saloon car engineer. Already renowned for its tractability, smoothness and lack of fuss, the Big Valve engine endows the car with a sparkling performance, particularly on acceleration, and the brakes are superb.

Although not the best there is, the gearchange is much improved, and the fifth gear gives relaxed cruising – something that the Lotus has always lacked.

But there is still much to criticise. Through no fault of their own, Lotus have had to offer the five-speed box with less than ideal ratios, the large gap between fourth and fifth being particularly noticeable. Strangely for a car from a specialist manufacturer with a long racing heritage – and despite continued criticism – the location of the major controls remains poor.

Our test car always started instantaneously from cold after giving the accelerator a few pumps. The only thing to tell you that the engine isn't fully warm is the temperature gauge for there is no temperament, missing, or lack of torque at low revs. Once warm the unit idles easily at about 600-700 rpm with only a slight lumpiness. Under power and at higher revs the unit feels smooth, although not as smooth as it does in the Elan; this can be directly attributed to the different and effectively harder engine mountings needed to stop the rear suspension moving about. The overall impression of refinement is vitiated a little, however, by the rorty note of the exhaust at town speeds and a slight boom between 5700 and 6000 rpm.

With a kerb weight of only 14 cwt and a healthy 126 bhp to push it along we expected excellent acceleration; even so we were pleasantly surprised at just how fast the Lotus is. From rest to 60 mph in a mere 6·6 sec would do credit to a sports car with three times the capacity. And it is not a 'speed-limit special' either, as it will go storming on past 70 mph with disdain. To reach 90 mph takes only 15·6 sec and it's only above this speed that the small engine begins to flag, especially on changing into fifth when you can feel the power die under the strain of the extra large gap between these two gears. However, it will still reach 100 mph in a creditable 21·6 sec.

One good result of the new gearbox is the improved cruising it brings. At 70 mph in fifth the engine is spinning at a mere 3400 rpm, while at 100 mph the revs rise to only 4900 rpm. It is possible to maintain 100 mph all day without any strain on the engine – or the driver. We were unable to substantiate Lotus' claim of a 125 mph maximum, though, perhaps because of the relative newness of the engine – it arrived with only 800 miles on the mileometer. The mean of opposite runs was 121·7 mph, with a best quarter of 123·3 mph – but we would expect this to increase as the engine loosened up.

Although the engine will pull from as little as 1000 rpm in fifth gear as long as the throttle is feathered (flooring the accelerator causes a slight fluffing between 1400 and 1800 rpm) there is little point in doing so. A drop down to fourth gear will reduce the 30-50 mph from a poor 12·6 sec to an excellent 6·3 sec.

Despite having a very high 10·3:1 compression ratio, the Europa Special is quite happy to run on normal premium fuel and showed no signs of pinking throughout the test. We achieved an overall fuel consumption of 24·2 mpg which is about average for the class. Our computed touring figure, however, is an excellent 33·1 mpg so more frugal drivers might be able to get around 30 mpg. The twin fuel tanks have a capacity of 12·5 gallons – a great improvement over the 7 gallons of the first Europa. Thus the maximum range possible would be an excellent 400 miles.

Before the advent of the R5, Renault gearchanges were not renowned for their slickness, and with the long linkage to the rear-sited Renault gearbox Lotus had more than their fair share of problems in making the Europa change work at all, let alone work well.

When we first drove the Special we were most unimpressed by the change; there was considerable friction in the linkage and the gears could be hard to find – especially when in a hurry. This was traced to a faulty biasing spring, however, and when we were able briefly to drive the car again we found the change to be excellent. The movements are short and the synchromesh unbeatable with only a trace of notchiness, into first. With stronger spring loading the precision was much improved and it was quite possible to go straight from fifth into first (for instance, when approaching traffic lights), something that had been very difficult with the box originally.

It is the poor gear ratios that are the weakest feature of the drive train. Intermediate maxima are 32, 49, 72 and 96 mph; if it were possible to pull 6500 rpm in fifth, the car would be doing a whopping 133 mph. The reason for these unusual ratios is cost

expediency; Lotus use the Renault 5-speed gearbox unchanged except for the fifth gear which they have made higher. Apparently the standard fifth gear ratio was not high enough for relaxed cruising, and to have changed the final drive ratio would have been too expensive. To be fair, however, the gaps in the ratios (apart from that between fourth and fifth) are effectively masked by the superb flexibility of the engine, and bottom is low enough for an easy restart on the 1-in-3 hill, which required little clutch slip.

We found this component to be almost perfect in its action, but subjectively it feels a lot heavier than its 37 lb release load might suggest, especially in traffic jams.

The steering, however, is very light, as well as direct and responsive, and even with the fat 175 HR 13 tyres fitted to the front wheels on our test car (an option, with 185 HR 13 tyres on the rear) it remained light when parking, one of the virtues of properly-designed mid-engined cars. Another such virtue is good roadholding which for the Europa is of such a high order that we doubt if there are more than a handful of cars that could keep up with a well-driven example on a winding road. Bumps in mid-corner don't throw it off line and it is virtually unaffected by cross winds.

To match this roadholding is handling that compares more than favourably with the best in the world. Like most mid-engined cars, the Europa understeers under power near the limit of adhesion; if you start to run wide or the corner tightens unexpectedly then the nose will tuck in on lifting the throttle, tightening your line. It does this so progressively and predictably that all that is normally needed from the driver is a slight reduction in lock. It is possible to corner in a much more flamboyant style, for there is more than enough engine power available to kick the back wheels out of line and hold the car in a stable opposite-lock slide.

With the excellent grip provided by the Firestone Cavallino tyres the Europa's servo-assisted disc/drum brakes sent the Tapley gauge soaring above 1·0 g with a pedal load of only 60 lb. A slight increase in pedal pressure was detected in our fade test on the third stop; after this things stabilised completely. A thorough soaking in the water-splash had no effect whatsoever.

These results are backed up by subjective impressions on the road. The brakes are extremely progressive and the feel is excellent. No amount of hard driving on the road caused the pedal pressure to rise, although the travel increased somewhat after a few brisk laps of MIRA's road circuit.

In contrast to the footbrakes, the handbrake is still rather pathetic. It would just hold the car on a 1-in-4 slope – a slight improvement over the original Europa – but was hopeless on a 1-in-3 slope. And it only managed a 0·24 g deceleration; very poor.

Getting into the low-slung Europa is not as difficult as it looks for the doors open widely.

Although the Europa looks quite small, it is in fact almost the same length and width as the larger-looking Porsche 914. In consequence, the room inside perhaps is more commodious than most people realise – our 6 ft 5 in beanpole managed to fit in very comfortably.

By using both the front and rear luggage compartments and squeezing one soft bag above the spare wheel we managed to fit in 4·8 cu ft of luggage. Care must be taken not to put any loose items in the front compartment for these can block the air flow both to the heater and to the fresh air vents.

Oddments space inside the car is rather sparse. There is only an open cubby in front of the passenger and two small pockets in the doors, each large enough for a couple of paperbacks.

Over practically all surfaces the Europa Special rides as well as a large saloon, let alone a light sports car with limited wheel travel. There is a trace of harshness at low speeds over small road disturbances such as cobbles when there is also some thump from the fat tyres. But generally the ride is good – firm but uncomfortable.

The Europa's seats gave plenty of side and lumbar support for most of our test staff, although one driver criticised them for lacking lumbar support on a long journey while another disliked the built-in headrests. Short drivers might find the low cushion restricts their rearward vision; an adjustable cushion would be a good thing, we feel.

There is plenty of fore and aft adjustment to suit the tallest of drivers and the relation between the seats, pedal, steering wheel and gearlever is very good. The centre console covering the backbone chassis and containing the gearlever is rather high though,

and the pedal layout is very poor. The brake has a lot of free travel and must be pressed beyond the accelerator during hard stops, so the only way you can heel-and-toe is to flick the accelerator with the side of your foot. A strange fault in a sports car.

Although the minor switches seem to be laid out for aesthetic appeal rather than function, they are fairly easy to use once their locations are memorised.

Despite rather thick screen pillars, visibility as far back as the rear edge of the doors is quite good, the short, low bonnet affording a good view of the road ahead. Rear-three-quarter vision was improved markedly earlier on in the Twin-Cam by cutting away the rear fins and all Europa Specials have outside mirrors as standard (the left one is useless except for left-hand drive cars). This does make vision to the rear more tolerable, except for short drivers.

The wipers clear enough windscreen area for tall drivers not to have to incline their heads to see out and the sealed-beam headlamps give a beam of excellent intensity and range.

Directly in front of the driver at the bottom of a fairly deep recess, are the rev counter and speedometer which are clearly calibrated, and free from unnecessary embellishments or reflections. Ranged above the radio on the centre console there are four supplementary dials (for fuel, water temperature, oil pressure and an ammeter) which although not in the normal line of sight are nevertheless easy to read.

Heating has never been one of the Europa's strong points and the Special is no better than its predecessors in this respect. In fact the system is rather primitive, the only controls being for temperature (mounted awkwardly on the centre console behind the gearlever and very sensitive and stiff in its action), flaps in the footwells to direct the air up or down, and a fan to boost the air flow. It is virtually impossible to maintain a stable temperature with this layout and, as we have already mentioned, flow can be completely blocked by soft luggage in the front compartment.

In contrast, the ventilation is very effective at all speeds, air being admitted to the interior via two eyeballs at each end of the facia. Luggage can block these too, though.

Except under hard acceleration at low road speeds, the Europa Special is not noisy for a highly tuned 1½-litre sports car. Under these conditions the rasping exhaust and engine boom period already mentioned are noticeable, but it is a pleasing noise and not obtrusive. There is some thump from the tyres over certain surfaces and a little whine from the gearbox in the intermediate ratios, but again the levels are low. Rather than cutting in suddenly at any one particular speed, wind noise gradually increases from about 70 mph until at about 95 mph it becomes fairly prominent.

Although the interior design gives the car an air of restrained opulence and a cursory glance might suggest a high standard of finish, there are quite a few shoddy areas.

Apart from these faults the interior is quite pleasing. Previously, Europas have had an all-enveloping black trim which has made the interior feel quite claustrophobic but our car was finished in the new optional beige colour which improved matters considerably. It made a good contrast to the external black and gold livery too.

Introduced in October 1972 and tested by *Motor* in January 1973, the Special was the ultimate development of the Europa. It continued in production until 1975. Its demise left a gap in Lotus' mid-engine range until the advent of the Esprit in October 1975 (see page 110).

GENERAL SPECIFICATION

Engine

Cylinders	4 in line, mid-mounted
Capacity	1558 cc
Bore/stroke	82·55 × 72·75 mm
Cooling	water
Block	cast iron
Head	alloy
Valves	dohc
Compression	10·3:1
Carburettor	2 Dellorto 40DHLA twin-choke
Bearings	5 main
Max power	126 bhp (DIN) at 6500 rpm
Max torque	113 lb-ft (DIN) at 5500 rpm

Transmission

Type	Renault 5-speed manual

Internal ratios and mph/1000 rpm

Top	0·87:1/20·4
4th	1·21:1/14·7
3rd	1·60:1/11·1
2nd	2·33:1/7·6
1st	3·62:1/4·9
Rev	3·08:1
Final drive	3·77:1

Body/Chassis

Construction	steel backbone chassis with reinforced glassfibre body

Suspension

Front	independent by wishbones, coil springs, anti-roll bar
Rear	independent by transverse links, radius arms, coil springs

Steering

Type	rack and pinion
Assistance	no

Brakes

Front	discs
Rear	drums
Servo	yes
Circuit	single

Wheels/Tyres

Type	alloy, 5½ × 13 in
Tyres	175/70-13 (front); 185/70-13 (rear)

Electrical

Battery	12v, 39 a-h
Earth	negative
Generator	alternator
Fuses	4
Headlights	2 × 75/50W

PERFORMANCE DATA

Maximum speeds

	mph	rpm
Top	121·7	5965
4th	96	6500
3rd	72	6500
2nd	49	6500
1st	32	6500

Acceleration from rest

mph	sec
0-30	2·2
0-40	3·3
0-50	4·8
0-60	6·6
0-70	9·0
0-80	11·8
0-90	15·6
0-100...	21·6
Standing ¼ mile	14·9
Standing km..	28·3

Acceleration in

mph	top sec	4th sec
20-40	12·1	6·6
30-50	12·6	6·3
40-60	11·8	6·0
50-70	11·5	5·6
60-80	11·5	5·9
70-90	12·3	6·7
80-100	14·1	8·5

Fuel consumption

Touring*	33·1 mpg
Overall	24·2 mpg
Tank capacity	12·5 gal
Max range	413 miles

*Consumption midway between 30 mph and maximum speed, less 5% allowance for acceleration.
Maximum range is based on touring consumption.

MASERATI Bora

With spare wheel removed there is a good view of the transmission and suspension

Despite some unusual Francophile refinements – a reflection of Masterati's erstwhile French owners – the Bora is what you might term modern Modenese of traditional ancestry; it was designed by the legendary Giulio Alfieri, the one important link left with the old Count Orsi-owned company after Citroen took over, and styled by Ital Design's Giugiaro. He dealt satisfactorily with the two Achilles' heels of the mid-engined layout – visibility and accommodation – within a dramatically smooth and elegant steel hull which does not sacrifice practicality to an unacceptable degree, for beauty. And beautiful it certainly is.

Power is from a four-cam V8 engine located lengthwise amidships, driving the rear wheels through a five-speed manual gearbox. Suspension is by coil and wishbone all round. There is a ventilated disc brake for each wheel.

The Bora's traction and (with reservations) braking and road-holding are everything you would expect of a well-shod mid-engined thoroughbred, and the performance is in the dragster class, with around 160 mph on tap. Even so, it must be said that you can buy similar performance and handling for two-thirds the price, so even for the very rich the Bora is a costly indulgence. But do not get us wrong; the Bora impressed us as one of the best and most civilised mid-engined exotics we have tried, better developed than most and immensely rewarding to drive, especially at speed on country roads. But if we are to be objective, the Bora's price tag does not spell value for money.

If a four-cam light-alloy Maserati V8 engine conjures impressions of ripped calico and peaky power, forget them. That of the Bora is just the opposite – silky smooth, unexpectedly quiet and almost as tractable as a steam engine. To start up you simply prime the four Weber carburettors with a few dabs on the throttle while the Bendix electric pump momentarily works overtime topping up the chambers, and then twist the key: the engine fires instantly on all eight cylinders, and idles and pulls cleanly immediately, although the handbook recommends that you do not move off straight away.

Maserati claim 310 bhp and a massive 339 lb-ft of torque from the well-developed 4·7-litre engine, impressive figures tempered only by the car's astonishingly high unladen weight of over 1½ tons, which must in part account for acceleration times that, while pretty staggering by normal standards, are by no means the quickest we have recorded.

Even so, from rest to 100 mph in under 15 sec is probably quick enough for most people and, more important, you can really use the acceleration without scaring anyone. Moreover, few cars can equal or better the Bora as an autostrada express. Excellent high-speed stability and low wind and engine noise make 130 mph seem little more than a canter on a Continental motorway.

Maserati claim a maximum speed of 170 mph but we believe this to be optimistic: claims for such exotica invariably are in our experience. To start with, this corresponds to an engine speed of 6 250 rpm even though the handbook rules that 6 000 rpm is the limit. In reality, we would say that given a long run-in, a genuine 5 700 rpm *might* be attainable in the very high fifth gear: that is 160 mph and we are probably being generous.

What did impress us, though, even more than the vicious acceleration and high cruising speed, was the quiet, fussless ease with which this performance was achieved. The engine pulls strongly from about 1 200 rpm without any snatch or fluffing, making the car, in third, virtually a one-gear automatic with a useable speed range of between 12 and 120 mph. Just as impressive as this excellent tractability is the lusty pull, devoid of any harsh boom or vibratory periods (although there is a more prominent mid-range burble). The power surges forth in a smooth, effortless flow, no matter what the engine speed (see how every 20 mph increase between 20 and 110 mph in fourth takes between six and seven seconds).

The Bora is a very thirsty car, regardless of how you drive it. Fast or (relatively) gentle progress did not seem to affect the fuel consumption significantly: all our spot checks showed it to be a little under 11 mpg.

The Bora's all-Italian power is fed through a British Borg and Beck clutch to a German ZF five-speed gearbox. At first, some drivers did not think it was a very happy marriage: indeed, we feel that some people would never come to terms with the inordinately heavy clutch action or a short, stout gear-lever that needs a firm hand to navigate it through a heavily spring-loaded gate. But once the necessary technique has been acquired and mastered – short, sharp movements of hand and foot – changing gear on the Bora becomes a pleasure to indulge. The lever has a short travel and unbeatable synchromesh that does not baulk or jar the movement so you can make, indeed are encouraged to make, the quick snap changes that the engine's low flywheel effect and close ratios demand.

On a twisty road the Bora has the sort of traction and squeal-less roll-free cornering power that you rarely encounter in a conventional front (or rear) engined road car. In these respects, let us call it grip, the mid-engined configuration is fully justified, especially on smooth, sweeping corners where the Bora reminded us strongly of the Ford GT40. You could unleash all the power on tap coming out of corners or roundabouts without breaking the grip of the monster 215/70 VR15 Michelin radial tyres, and on smooth corners you would have to be very brave (or foolish) to reach the exceptionally high limit. We had to experiment at MIRA to discover that at the sort of g forces you are unlikely to encounter on the road the car is actually quite sensitive to throttle opening: lift off in mid corner and the nose tucks in, turn on the power and understeer sets in again. Of course, the tail will step out of line if you provoke it in the wet, but it does so in a commendably controllable way.

Despite its tenacious bond with the road, however, we cannot credit the Bora with five-star handling, largely because it can become quite a handful to hold on course when driving briskly on secondary roads. The firm, jiggly suspension is very sensitive to bumps and camber changes so the car tends to dart and meander on poor roads. Usually, it is all self-correcting but every now and then it is not and you have to twitch the car back on course.

On the move, the rack and pinion steering is light and responsive, even though not especially high geared. It also feeds to the driver very strong messages about what's happening at the front, writhing, sometimes kicking quite strongly in your hands. When manoeuvring, however, the steering is heavy and ponderous.

A balanced assessment of braking is difficult. The reason is that the objectively measured figures, not known to most drivers when they filed their reports, are far better than subjective assessment led them to believe. In other words the brakes don't *feel* very powerful when in fact they are: put to

the ultimate test of anchoring the car quickly and safely from 150 mph, they really come up trumps.

Citroen drivers will probably feel at home straight away because there's a lot of Citroen know-how and hardware in the Bora's all-ventilated disc brakes. Pushing the brake pedal, which is sensitive more to pressure than movement (it hardly gives at all), merely taps energy from a high-pressure hydraulic circuit, pressurised by an engine-driven pump. At low speeds, we found it virtually impossible to 'feather' the brakes on, although they responded progressively enough to additional pressure once the pads had been snapped into contact with the discs. Around town, a light caress on the pedal was sufficient to stop the car. At speed, much higher pedal loads were required, creating an impression sometimes that the brakes were fading. In fact they were not. Hard high-speed braking also induced a disquieting rumble which, in fairness, did not seem to impair braking efficiency. Our 20-stop test at minute intervals from over 100 mph produced no fade at all. Nor did two much harder stops from 130 mph immediately afterwards: the Bora stopped all square, albeit rumbling loudly, with the Tapley meter soaring to over 1 g.

The handbrake, in contrast, was pretty feeble. As an emergency form of braking it was useless, although with twin divided circuits no one should ever have to resort to a handbrake stop; as a hill anchor it is not much better

Mid-engined cars do not have to be cramped, as the abortive Rover BS prototype proved. The Bora, to a lesser extent, under-lines the point, even though there is a lot of wasted space above the engine. Drivers up to six feet in height should have adequate head and legroom but because the battery box intrudes into the other footwell, tall passengers have to sit with their knees up. People who could extend their legs to the toeboard found the Bora a very comfortable car to ride in. Luggage accommodation in the front boot is surprisingly generous, but stowage space inside the cockpit is un-necessarily mean.

More than one driver observed that the Bora would have been a better car with Citroen suspension rather like Citroen brakes. As it is, nothing could be less Citroen-like than the Maserati's stiff coil and wish-bone set-up, which is uncompromisingly firm. On indifferent roads, all the bumps get through as a restless jiggle which could be pretty uncomfortable, especially at low speed. Seldom does the suspension jolt badly or crash over really deep depressions though, suggesting good insulation between suspension and chassis if not much resilience in the springs.

The same high-pressure hydraulics that operate the brakes also power the pedal assembly and seat. The seat is rigidly fixed in the fore and aft plane but can be tilted about its front mounting to raise the eye level of very short drivers. The pedals rush to and fro at the touch of the other adjustment lever on the facia. The system is excellent but the range of adjustment is not great enough for tall drivers.

In addition, the steering column can be telescoped and adjusted for height (both manually) and it was here, rather than at the seat or pedals, that most of us were able to make the fine adjustments necessary for at least a tolerable driving position – and in some cases a very good one.

The pleated seats, rather hammock-like in shape, do not look all that inviting although one driver described them as 'the best I've ever sat in'. He was on his own. Comfort depended most on whether you could get your thighs down onto the front of the cushion: only those who could remained relaxed and comfortable on long journeys.

Most of the controls are well placed, the pedals being properly aligned at the same height for easy heel and toe changes. The rest to the left of the clutch is pretty useless, unless you have very small, dainty feet. Fingertip stalks operate the two-speed wipers, washers, indicators, dip and (curiously) the interior light.

You get a splendid view of the road ahead through the massive, steeply raked screen, although parking and turning manoeuvres are not so easy as you cannot see the front corners: even when sitting up (which the low roof does not really allow) the parked wipers get in the way. Visibility aft in the dipping mirror is also quite good, although the sloping rear canopy and double glazed partition ahead of it, not to say misplaced imprinted labels on both, blurr the image somewhat. Rear three-quarter visibility is not so good and it helps to make right-angle approaches at oblique junctions to see what's coming.

The two-speed wipers sweep a good area of glass and do not lift off at speed.

The headlights pop up automatically (under hydraulic power again) when switched on but they are not much use for flashing unless they are left in the raised position. In fact they are not much use for night driving either, which is surprising when you consider the magnificent searchlights that Citroen fit to their own cars.

Nothing is lacking on the instrument panel, at least not in quantity. There are eight dials altogether, two big ones for the speedometer and rev counter with an oil pressure gauge in between, and five others, angled inwards from the centre console to minimise parallax error. All are clearly calibrated although the small figures and delicate pointers of the smaller instruments are difficult to read when your jowls are a-quiver on secondary roads. It needs more than a cursory glance in such conditions.

Our test car was fitted with air conditioning. That it works is all we are prepared to say since we could hardly assess its worth in the cold spell that prevailed throughout our test. The heating and ventilation did not impress us at all.

To start with, it takes some time after a cold start for warm air to filter through the rather cheap-looking flap valves which can be twisted and aimed in most directions. Response to adjustment of the temperature control is rather slow and some drivers also complained that their right foot got left out in the cold. Even so, the heater does a satisfactory job given time, but there is no separate ventilation system so you cannot aim cool air at your face while warming the footwells.

The double glazing of the bulkhead is presumably largely responsible for isolating engine noise so well from the cockpit. Wind noise is also low, the gearbox reasonably quiet (although the indirect ratios do whine) and the structure comendably free from squeaks, rattles and crashing noises. What disturbs the peace most is road roar on a coarse surface, although on smooth roads,

this noise reduces to a swish and more acceptable proportions.

The decor inside, though finished in high quality materials, is nothing very special: black leather upholsters most surfaces and there's a dust-collecting covering of felt atop the facia. The exterior finish we thought was rather more impressive, especially the deep lustre of the paint and the stainless steel roof.

In 1979 the Bora was still essentially unchanged, but with the engine uprated to 4 930 cc (320 bhp) and suspension changes which are claimed to have improved roadholding. Although Maserati's link with Citroen ended in 1975 (it was taken over by de Tomaso) the Citroen-type high-pressure hydraulic braking system is still fitted.

GENERAL SPECIFICATION

Engine

Cylinders	8 in vee
Capacity	4 719 cc
Bore/stroke	93·9 × 85 mm
Cooling	water
Block	alloy
Head	alloy
Valves	dohc per bank
Compression	8·5:1
Carburettor	4 Weber 42DCNF twin-choke
Bearings	5 main
Max power	310 bhp (DIN) at 6 000 rpm
Max torque	339 lb-ft (DIN) at 4 200 rpm

Transmission

Type	ZF 5-speed manual
Internal ratios and mph/1000 rpm	
Top	0·740:1/28·0
4th	0·846:1/24·5
3rd	1·040:1/19·9
2nd	1·520:1/13·7
1st	2·580:1/8·0
Rev	2·86:1
Final drive	3·77:1

Body/Chassis

Construction	integral steel body/chassis with separate subframes, front and rear

Suspension

Front	independent by coil springs and wishbones, telescopic dampers, anti-roll bar
Rear	independent by coil springs and wishbones, telescopic dampers, anti-roll bar

Steering

Type	rack and pinion
Assistance	no

Brakes

Front	11 in ventilated discs
Rear	11 in ventilated discs
Servo	Citroen-type high-pressure hydraulic system
Circuit	split

Wheels/Tyres

Type	alloy, 7½ × 15 in
Tyres	Michelin 215/70 VR15

Electrical

Battery	12v, 72 a-h
Earth	negative
Generator	alternator
Fuses	4
Headlights	2 quartz halogen

PERFORMANCE DATA

Maximum speeds

	mph	rpm
Top (estimated) ...	160	5700
4th	147	6000
3rd	120	6000
2nd	82	6000
1st	48	6000

Acceleration from rest

mph	sec
0-30	2·5
0-40	3·3
0-50	5·1
0-60	6·5
0-70	8·0
0-80	9·9
0-90	12·4
0-100...	14·7
0-110...	17·9
0-120...	23·0
Standing ¼ mile	14·6
Standing km..	26·2

Acceleration in

mph	top sec	4th sec
20-40	—	6·6
30-50	7·7	6·7
40-60	7·7	6·2
50-70	7·5	6·0
60-80	7·3	6·1
70-90	7·6	6·2
80-100	8·4	6·2
90-110	8·8	6·8
100-120	10·1	8·6

Fuel consumption

Touring (estimated)*	11·0 mpg
Overall	10·9 mpg
Tank capacity	19·8 gal
Max range	220 miles

*Consumption midway between 30 mph and maximum speed less 5% allowance for acceleration. Maximum range is based on touring consumption.

PANTHER J72

The Panther's Jaguar V12 engine with six twin-choke carburettors

'Claret is the liquor for boys; port for men; but he who aspires to be a hero must drink brandy,' said Dr Johnson, but if a time machine could transport you back to his table, might you not find your appreciation of his wit somewhat spoiled by the dirtiness of his eating habits? We advance the proposition in support of our belief that nostalgia is essentially a specious emotion which blinds one to the unpleasantnesses of the past. There is no doubt, for instance, that some of the cars built in the 1920s and 1930s were among the most beautiful to look at ever conceived, and for this reason they rightly continue to excite almost universal admiration. Equally, there is no doubt that nearly all such classic cars would be considered grotesquely inadequate by modern standards in virtually every important aspect of design.

Take performance, for example – and try reading some pre-war *Motor* road tests: it is a saddening experience. Maximum speeds of over 100 mph and 0-60 mph acceleration times of less than 15 sec were exceptional, even for the most exotic and glamorous models. As for handling and roadholding, we well remember our former Editor, Charles Bulmer, telling us of an occasion in the late 1950s when he was easily able to keep up with a friend in his sporting Bugatti while driving an absolutely standard Issigonis Morris Minor. In their heating, ventilation and visibility, most vintage models are also disasters; in their ride, too, if they are sports cars.

But we have had the good fortune to drive one car which combined the classic beauty of appearance with all the period character, but which lacked some of the more important drawbacks – and had far more performance than any vintage sports car ever had. This was the Panther, a modern, superbly finished vehicle which is not so much a replica as an evocation of the Jaguar SS 100 first introduced in 1935. Normally it is available with the standard Jaguar 4·2 litre six-cylinder or 5·4 litre V12 engines, but ours was a special version, its V12 sporting six twin-choke Weber carburettors in place of the usual four Stromberg instruments.

If the Panther is a remarkable car it is because it was created by a remarkable man: Robert Jankel, designer and business-man. Many years ago Robert worked in the tuning business but "I found I couldn't make a living at it," so he left to join the textile industry, eventually becoming chief exec-utive and a major shareholder in a company employing 400 people. Throughout this period of advancement, however, Bob Jankel maintained one important hobby, the design and building of a succession of specials – not all vintage in style and concept – at the rate of about one per year, culminat-ing in the Panther.

In 1971 he sold out his textile interests leaving him 'with quite a lot of money' and time on his hands – so what more natural than to invest a bit of both in the production of Panthers on a regular basis, as the original prototype excited a good deal of interest and some orders. Since starting in his own (but well equipped) garage, he has moved into a proper little factory and has bought up some of the small companies to whom in the old days as an amateur he used to farm out work such as panel beating and trimming. The resultant small group now do subcontract work for outsiders like Rolls-Royce, build two or three Panthers a week (mostly Jaguar-based J72s rather than the Ferrari-based FF) and have time to create the occasional styling exercise like the Lazer Sport.

In construction as well as style the Panther uses many techniques typical of the 1930s, having a flimsy-looking chassis very similar to the SS100's except that its members are of box section. And the all-aluminium body is not supported by an ash frame, but by extensions from the chassis – two large ones support the front wings, for example – and by a framework of square steel tube. At the front this is sufficiently extensive to brace the scuttle, but does not extend rearwards through the door apertures and so contri-butes relatively little to the overall torsional stiffness.

If up-to-date fabrication methods are used

to advantage in places, the tubular beam front axle is uncompromisingly vintage, although its Formula 1 type coil spring-damper units and its excellent location – by parallel radius arms and a Panhard rod – are, again, modern. The beam terminates in the well-proven axle ends/kingpin carriers of the Ford Transit van, but the hubs carry massive Jaguar disc brakes. The steering is a straightforward recirculating ball system.

Set well back in the chassis to clear this beam axle, the V12 engine drives through a standard XJ6/E-type gearbox (as do the six-cylinder versions) and a short propeller shaft to a Salisbury live axle on coil springs. It is located by parallel radius arms and a short, angled Panhard rod in a layout similar to an old Jaguar arrangement. Disc brakes are also fitted at the rear.

But all this tells only half the story, for one of the most striking features of the Panther is its exquisite workmanship. This is not limited to the accuracy of the bodywork curves or the deep gloss of the paintwork but extends to the most minor details of which the most striking is the chrome plating of all the front radius arms and steering links with their specially bushed Rose joints which need no lubrication (though they squeak a bit at times). At the end of our test we could fault the car on only a few minor points like a faulty glovebox lock.

It is perhaps this manifest quality of workmanship as much as the striking appearance which makes the Panther such a friend-maker. Shopping with the Panther reminded us of the days back in the 1950s when interesting and unusual motor cars abounded and a half-minute of appreciative kerbside inspection was all the introduction their owners needed. During the course of a single weekend we chatted to the driver of a Morgan, a motorcyclist (whose mount would 'only' get to 60 mph from a standstill in about 8 sec) and many others. All expressed unqualified admiration for the car, which never, incidentally, became tinged with disapproval when told of the performance

figures or with envy when told of the price.

Exactly why the Panther provided the most enjoyable motoring we have had for years is not quite so easily stated. The tremendous performance helped, of course, but we will come to that later. It was perhaps the way it managed to be utterly vintage in character – complete with carburettor hissings, engine smells, a multiplicity of creaks and rattles and a ride on bumpy surfaces that felt as if it would destroy the car – yet with the faults sufficiently tamed to make it drivable at very high speeds indeed. Its steering and road-holding were vastly superior to those of an original SS100 that we drove some years ago, as were its brakes: however good in this respect the Jaguar may have been in its day, there is nothing like a good servo-assisted set of modern disc brakes for inspiring confidence.

The steering, too, inspired confidence, even though it suffered from two faults typical of some pre-war sports cars: an appallingly poor lock – although better than the SS100's – and a tendency to tighten up at the extremes of movement. It was very heavy at parking speeds also, but became light on the move, was direct, and – unlike many vintage systems – pretty accurate as well, while lacking that complete freedom from any perceptible play which is the hallmark of the best modern rack and pinion systems. In conjunction with the lack of roll, the stiffness of the springs and the total absence of suspension compliance, this gave the Panther the overall responsiveness and go-where-you-point-it precision of handling about which vintage enthusiasts so often eulogise.

But the real truth is that in most such cars on all but completely smooth surfaces the driver was constantly and anxiously sawing at the wheel in order to cope with the slack in the steering and the shimmying of the front axle – anyone who has driven a beam-axled van or motor caravan on a French road with crumbling edges will know the sensation. The big surprise, then, was to find the Panther largely free of these faults. On smooth surfaces – such as those of highways – it remained stable up to about 120 mph before starting to weave a little and on rough ones to about 110 mph. Moreover, it was not often put off line by bumps and so could be driven really quickly on twisty country roads.

But, of course, it had its limits. It could not be driven as quickly as a good modern sports car of the Dino or Elan sort. Try to step over those limits and it would start to jump from bump to bump and weave about in an alarming way. And even below them it was a pretty wearing business. In fact, the scuttle and wings did not shake about much, but everything else did, particularly the side-screens, and the ride, full of violent high-

frequency, small amplitude pitchings and bouncings, although just tolerable on smooth roads, became positively hysterical on rough ones.

Most of the time all we had to do was turn the wheel and point the car, but at higher cornering speeds mild understeer was noticeable. But put down some power and the behaviour becomes neutral; more still – a lot more – and the car oversteers gently, seldom wagging its tail or acquiring much of an attitude angle, thanks to an extremely effective limited-slip differential. The same component made driving the Panther in the wet a surprisingly trauma-free experience, despite the enormous power and torque available: during one torrential downpour the car's main fault was excessive sensitivity to puddles.

But perhaps the Panther's greatest charm was its mind-blowing acceleration. With six Weber carburettors instead of four Stromberg instruments and about 450 lb less weight than a V12 E-type, it does not quite fulfill its promise but up to about 100 mph is nevertheless significantly quicker than the Jaguar and one of the fastest cars we have had in its capacity class, barring one or two league-table freaks. Above that speed wind resistance begins to take its toll, although it would comfortably pull 6000 rpm in top while still accelerating and so should be able to achieve a maximum of about 140 mph at 6500 rpm.

There are some drawbacks, though – apart from the 8 mpg overall fuel consumption. In its E-type application the engine will pull like a train from 600 rpm, but Panther-style it gulps and staggers if you floor the throttle at low rpm and will not pull at all until around 30 mph in top. And at about 2500 rpm a loud boom issues from the four separate exhaust pipes on a trailing throttle which changes to a disorganised staggering throb when the throttle is open. Under all other conditions, however, the engine emitted a magnificent creamy blare and sounded completely unperturbed even at its 6500 rpm limit. Once we had got the measure of the power and adjusted our eyes to the effect it would produce, we never tired of dropping down to second or third – when top would have been enough to annihilate everything within sight – and crushing the accelerator to the floor just to eat up the long straight ahead.

Whereas we can hardly get our legs beneath the wheel of an SS100, the Panther has a sensible modern driving position with plenty of legroom and a comfortable seat which has a reclining backrest. The soft top was very easy to erect and its Velcro seals remained substantially draughtproof up to about 90 mph when they tended to pop loose here and there. Even in the hot weather which mostly prevailed during our test, the breeze through the small sliding windows in the sidescreens maintained the interior reasonably cool on the move. But with the soft top erect the three-quarter rear visibility is very poor and the rudimentary heating system could not prevent all the windows from misting up in the rain. The resultant claustrophobia made us realise more than anything how much car design has advanced since 1935. However, the Panther is a splendid toy if you have the asking price to spare.

The V12 version of the Panther J72 that *Motor* tested was one of just 12 cars built with the V12 power unit, and was unique in having the Weber six-carburettor conversion; the remaining 11 were equipped with the then-standard Stromberg four-carburettor layout. The J72 remains in production, however, with the standard 4235cc (193 bhp) Jaguar six-cylinder in-line engine.

GENERAL SPECIFICATION

Engine
Cylinders	12 in vee
Capacity	5343 cc
Bore/stroke	90 × 70 mm
Cooling	water
Block	alloy
Head	alloy
Valves	sohc per bank
Compression	9:1
Carburettor	6 Weber 40DCI
Bearings	7 main
Max power	not quoted
Max torque	not quoted

Transmission
Type	Jaguar 4-speed manual

Internal ratios and mph/1000 rpm
Top	1·00:1/21·6
3rd	1·389:1/15·6
2nd	1·905:1/11·3
1st	2·933:1/7·2
Rev	3·378:1
Final drive	4·92:1

Body/Chassis
Construction	separate steel chassis, aluminium body panels on steel frame

Suspension
Front	live axle on coil springs located by parallel radius arms and Panhard rod
Rear	live axle on coil springs located by parallel radius arms and Panhard rod

Steering
Type	recirculating ball
Assistance	no

Brakes
Front	10·6 in discs
Rear	11·4 in discs
Servo	yes
Circuit	split

Wheels/Tyres
Type	wire spoke, 6J × 15 in
Tyres	ER70 VR15

Electrical
Battery	12v , 60 a-h
Earth	negative
Generator	60 amp alternator
Fuses	11
Headlights	Panther-Cibié

PERFORMANCE DATA

Maximum speeds		mph	rpm
Top (estimated)	...	140	6500
3rd	...	101	6500
2nd	...	73	6500
1st	...	47	6500

Acceleration from rest
mph					sec
0-30	...	...	...	....	2·4
0-40	...	...	...	....	3·3
0-50	...	...	...	....	4·5
0-60	...	...	...	....	5·7
0-70	...	...	...	....	7·4
0-80	...	...	...	....	9·2
0-90	...	...	...	....	11·1
0-100	...	...	...	....	13·8
0-110	...	...	...	....	18·2
0-120	...				. —
Standing ¼ mile		...	....		14·3
Standing km...			....		26·6

Acceleration in
mph				top sec
10-30	.	...	...	—
20-40	.	...	...	—
30-50	.	...	...	4·9
40-60	.	...	...	4·7
50-70	.	...	...	4·5
60-80	.	...	...	4·3
70-90	.	...	...	5·3
80-100	.	...	...	6·0
90-110	.	...	...	7·2
100-120	.	...	...	

Fuel consumption
Touring*	12·0 mpg
Overall	9·6 mpg
Tank capacity	28 gal
Max range	336 miles

*Consumption midway between 30 mph and maximum speed less 5% allowance for acceleration. Maximum range is based on touring consumption.

MASERATI Khamsin

Maserati, Ferrari and Lamborghini are three Italian companies whose impact on the motoring scene is almost ridiculously out of all proportion to the number of cars they make. In absolute terms their output is infinitesimal: yet there cannot be many who have not heard the names or who do not hanker after their products. To the majority of the public they symbolise cars that are immensely fast, beautifully styled (probably by one of the famous coachbuilders) with superb road manners and all the right technical specifications. In our experience they do not all live up to this image, but the Maserati Merak (among others) did, so we looked forward to trying the first right-hand-drive Khamsin but tempered our enthusiasm a little just in case.

At the time of our test the range consisted of the mid-engined Merak and Bora, the front-wheel-drive four-door Quattroporte II, and the front-engined rear-wheel-drive Indy and Khamsin. The Bora, Indy and Khamsin all shared a big V8 engine, but with a capacity of 4719 cc in the Bora and 4931 cc (plus a little more power) in the other two. Compared with the Indy the Khamsin was a more compact 2 + 2, with independent rear suspension instead of a live axle, and is a later car altogether, having made its debut (in prototype form) at Turin in 1972.

Bertone was responsible for the low all-steel monocoque bodywork, and the shape is spectacular, to put it mildly, attracting enormous attention whether on the move or standing still. The 4·9 litre all-alloy V8 breathes in through four twin-choke downdraught Weber carburettors, and has twin overhead camshafts to each bank. It produces a generous 316 bhp (DIN) at a fairly conservative 5500 rpm, and a thumping 354 lb-ft (DIN) torque at 4000 rpm, a high speed for such a relatively big, low-revving engine.

A ZF manual gearbox is standard equipment but our test car was fitted with the optional extra Borg-Warner AS6 8N three-speed and torque convertor automatic. The 3·07:1 limited slip differential fitted to cars with automatic boxes gives a top gear figure of 25·5 mph/1000 rpm, thus effectively setting the top speed of 140 mph, corresponding to the red-lined 5500 maximum rpm.

The suspension is independent all round, with twin wishbones, coil springs, telescopic dampers and an anti-roll bar at the front, and a similar set-up at the back but with the exception that there are four (two each side) coil spring/damper units: the whole of the rear suspension and the differential are mounted on a separate sub-frame, and can be quickly removed.

Both the rack and pinion steering and the ventilated disc brake set-up are fully powered, via Citroen's unique system, but Maserati have not gone as far as hydropneumatic suspension.

In absolute terms the Khamsin's straight-line performance is way above average, but it is not as quick as might be expected from the specification. In addition to the power-robbing accessories, the automatic transmission and the high all-up weight (32 cwt) tend to drag the acceleration down to a point where it is only just competitive with that of the Jensen Interceptor (which also has automatic transmission). The fat tyres, MIRA's

ultra-grippy surface and a high peak torque speed plus the fact that the engine was only pulling about 2500 rpm at full stall during our standing start tests, meant that it was impossible to spin the wheels for a really good 0 to 60 mph time. Subjectively, too, the engine does not really begin to pull all that strongly until about 3500 rpm, which compounded the problem, so that at low revs the Khamsin is a little disappointing.

From this point on, though, power comes surging in smoothly and rapidly in a very satisfying manner. Thus the Maserati scores at high speeds and revs. Compared with the Interceptor again the times from 30 to 50 mph in kickdown are identical (2·7 sec) but from 70 to 90 mph the Khamsin is pulling away strongly, taking only 4·1 sec for this speed increment as against the Jensen's 6·2 sec, and from 100 to 120 mph it is over 3 sec quicker 10·6 sec against 14·0 sec: but neither car is on a par with the manual transmission Aston Martin, which takes only 6·8 sec for the last speed increase.

The somewhat academic question of the maximum speeds is a little confusing. Strictly speaking, with the 3·07:1 rear axle ratio, it is rev-limited to 140 mph at 5500 rpm, the peak of the power curve and also where the red line starts on the tachometer. But the handbook says only that it is not *recommended* to run for long periods above this speed, and goes on to indicate that 6000 rpm is feasible, a speed which corresponds to 152 mph. However, 140 mph is probably quite fast enough for most people, and we doubt that anyone would be prepared to run for any length of time with the tacho needle in the red band anyway.

The engine itself is untemperamental in action, starting easily after the usual (for cars equipped with Weber carburettors) couple of pumps on the accelerator pedal. On the other hand our test car was very noisy when accelerating hard, and there was a particularly irritating exhaust boom period at about 2000 rpm, or 50 mph in top, which the glass tail seemed to accentuate rather than subdue, and which made travelling around town or gently on the open road very tiring. The engine also tended to splutter a little with small throttle openings below 1500 rpm, and was rough at idle, with a continuous slight shake. On the other hand the engine noises die away at higher speeds, and it is much quieter and smoother when running between 70 and 100 mph. We must point out, however, that another privately-owned left-hand drive but later example that we tried was very much better in this respect – the boom was still there, but not so pronounced, while the noise on acceleration was probably no less but was much more crisp and pleasant.

With this sort of car, and an automatic gearbox as well, you do not expect very good fuel consumption, and the Khamsin's overall figure of 12·8 mpg is poor by absolute standards but about average for this class of car. Strangely enough the touring fuel consumption gave a notably flat curve, starting at 19·6 mpg at 30 mph, and staying over 20 mpg at 40, 50 and 60 mph – and then only falling gradually to 16·5 mpg at 100 mph.

The Borg-Warner automatic transmission used for the Khamsin is an old-fashioned unit, with the now obsolete L/D1/D2 change pattern. With this configuration D1 is used for normal running, when the transmission will start in first and move up through the gears: L is to hold first only, and D2 cuts out first. Holding first until 5500 rpm did not improve on the acceleration times in D1, but using D2 only, not unnaturally, meant slower acceleration times, 60 mph from a standstill for example taking 10·8 sec. There is no way of holding second, but full-throttle changes from this gear to third occurred at 5300 rpm, an indicated 93 mph. The later cars, however, have a more normal D-2-1 arrangement.

The changes themselves were very smooth, even on full throttle, where only a slight check and a change in engine note were any indication that they had taken place. The transmission felt a little reluctant to kick down, but this may be just an impression created by the heavy pedal pressures for the second part of the accelerator travel: again the later model was very much more responsive and willing, and without the high pedal loads.

Even now, some years after it was introduced, the powered steering system pioneered by Citroen and fitted to their products as well as the Khamsin arouses controversy. It does take some getting used to, but once you have, anything else seems cumbersome and ponderous. At first it feels impossibly direct and sensitive, so that at low speeds and around town you tend to take corners in a series of 'bites', and generally follow a rather erratic course, but after a while you get used to it. Once you do it is superb especially on the open road, since power assistance and hence over-sensitivity decreases as speed increases and it becomes delightfully direct and accurate. The wide 70-series Michelin XWX tyres have tremendeous adhesion, the car feels beautifully balanced, and the Khamsin is a fabulous machine on medium-speed or fast sweeping curves, with a go-where-it's-pointed neutral attitude, and negligible roll. On the other hand the harsh ride means that roadholding on bumpy surfaces is distinctly poor, although this may be compounded by the fact that the bumps cause your arms to jerk, and this in turn leads to a twitch at the steering wheel.

Like the steering the brakes take some learning. At high speeds they are superb,

feeling immensely powerful and progressive. But at low speeds, and when it is least expected, you can lock up the wheels ludicrously easily – the dividing line between hard braking and lock-up is far too fine. The same is true but much more pronounced in the wet – it is essential to brake in a straight line and be prepared for lock-up

The luggage accommodation is generous for this class of car, with a large, flat, usefully-shaped and carpeted compartment behind the rear seats, accessible through the wide-opening tail-gate. Without them coming above window level 8·9 cu ft of suitcases filled this area – more could be carried at the expense of some rearward vision. Passenger space in the rear, on the other hand, is really limited to children for there is a severe shortage of head, leg and foot-room, even with the front seat well forward.

One of the less pleasant features of the Khamsin is the ride. It is harsh and jiggly at low speeds (enough to blur the exterior mirror), there is a lot of small-bump harshness which makes even smooth highways feel lumpy, and over poor quality roads it is sufficiently turbulent to affect the handling: surprisingly enough it takes long wave undulations and hump-back bridges extremely well.

The seat is adjustable fore-and-aft and it can be tilted hydraulically via a little rocking lever on the floor, while the steering column, too, is adjustable for reach and rake, so a reasonably comfortable driving position is easily found. We felt, however, that the seat itself was too hard and uncomfortable, lacking in lateral support, and there is not nearly enough headroom for tall drivers.

The major controls are fairly well located, with plenty of foot-room around the pedals (which are set up for either left or right foot braking) and there is a left foot brace too. The handbrake, though, is too close to the transmission tunnel, so you can catch your knu-

ckles, but the worst feature by far is the very poor minor controls. These are thoroughly confusing, badly located and scattered and often not clearly labelled – recourse to the handbook helps a little, but this, of curse, refers only to left-hand-drive cars. For example the stalk to operate the lights on left-hand-drive cars simply works the interior light on right-hand drive models, and the wiper delay switch is a stretch away on the left of the dashboard.

The same comments apply to the temperature controls, which are also scattered amongst the others. Once the system is learnt, however, it proves effective. In cold conditions the heater output is ample and controllable, while unseasonable warm weather and the hot-house effect from the considerable glass area showed that the conditioning system, too, worked well, although we wonder whether it would cope with really hot situations.

Most of the instruments (speedometer, fuel, oil pressure and water temperature gauges and tachometer) are grouped in a panel in front of the driver, only the battery condition indicator, clock and oil temperature gauges finding a home in the centre console. Unfortunately the 40 mph to 100 mph sector of the speedometer is hidden by the rim of the steering wheel, as is the fuel gauge. All the dials are white on black and look attractive, but those in the centre console are not too visible, and none are well calibrated. The speedometer was remarkably accurate.

The major source of noise is the engine and its ancillaries, for apart from the rumble of the exhaust there are other assorted engine compartment noises (including an occasional clonk from the air conditioning pump), some creaks and groans from the suspension, fairly high road noise which is very noticeable on coarse surfaces, and some transmission whine. At higher speeds, though, the engine fuss recedes and wind noise is well suppressed, so the Khamsin can then become a quite civilised high-speed machine.

For a car costing so much the finish was not impressive. The windscreen pillar trim was badly glued in place, the rear window catch was very stiff, the seat-back loose on its mountings, the front bumper was misaligned, and various electrical faults appeared – the electric window/rear screen heater fuse kept blowing, the wipers would not switch off except by removing a fuse, and the light switch was erratic. In addition we thought the hinges for the tailgate which protrude into the passenger space looked clumsy, and the plastic air vents cheap, but on the other hand the finish of the seats and other leather-work was good, and we liked the velvet finish to the dashboard top. Again the later car had a considerably better finish.

Looking over your shoulder the visibility through the glass tail is about the best there is, but the mirrors (both internal and external) are too small, and a high waistline and long sloping nose can make parking tricky.

The only extras that a potential owner might like to specify that we can think of are a radio and a sun roof: the standard list includes air conditioning, leather upholstery, variable ratio power steering, power brakes, tinted glass, electric windows and a heated rear screen.

The Maserati Khamsin remains in production virtually unchanged, retaining its Citroen-type steering and high-pressure

Citroen ended in the autumn of 1975 when the company was taken over by the de Tomaso organization.

Centre, left:
Vision to the rear is excellent thanks to the glass tail

GENERAL SPECIFICATION

Engine

Cylinders	8 in vee
Capacity	4930 cc
Bore/stroke	93·9 × 89 mm
Cooling	water
Block	alloy
Head	alloy
Valves	dohc per bank
Compression	8·5:1
Carburettor	4 Weber 42DCNF twin-choke
Bearings	5 main
Max power	316 bhp (DIN) at 5 500 rpm
Max torque	354 lb-ft (DIN) at 4 000 rpm

Transmission

Type	Borg-Warner 3-speed automatic

Internal ratios and mph/1000 rpm

Top	1·00:1	25·5
2nd	1·47:1	17·3
1st	2·40:1	10·6
Rev	2·00:1	
Final drive	3·07:1	

Body/Chassis

Construction	integral, steel

Suspension

Front	independent by wishbones, coil springs, anti-roll bar
Rear	independent by wishbones, twin coil spring/damper units, anti-roll bar

Steering

Type	rack and pinion
Assistance	yes

Brakes

Front	10·75 in ventilated discs
Rear	10·30 in ventilated discs
Servo	high-pressure hydraulic
Circuit	dual

Wheels/Tyres

Type	alloy, 7½J × 15 in
Tyres	Michelin 215 VR15

Electrical

Battery	12v, 60 a-h
Earth	negative
Generator	alternator
Fuses	16
Headlights	4 quartz halogen

PERFORMANCE DATA

Maximum speeds	mph	rpm
Top	140	5 490
2nd	95	5 500
1st	58	5 500

Acceleration from rest

mph	sec
0-30	3·5
0-40	4·6
0-50	6·2
0-60	7·9
0-70	9·8
0-80	12·2
0-90	14·9
0-100	19·9
0-110	24·9
0-120	30·5
Standing ¼ mile	15·6
Standing km	30·0

Acceleration in kickdown

mph	sec
10-30	—
20-40	—
30-50	2·7
40-60	3·3
50-70	3·6
60-80	4·3
70-90	5·1
80-100	7·7
90-100	10·0
100-120	10·6

Fuel consumption

Touring*	16·8 mpg
Overall	12·8 mpg
Tank capacity	19·8 gal
Max range	332 miles

*Consumption midway between 30 mph and maximum speed less 5% allowance for acceleration.
Maximum range is based on touring consumption.

LAMBORGHINI Urraco

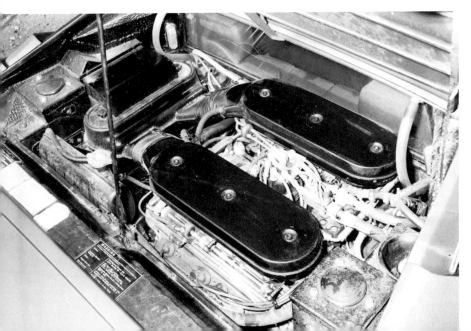

For the price of a car like the Lamborghini Urraco P300 you could buy a suburban property or half a dozen Iron Curtain cars. Or more realistically you could buy a 150 mph Porsche Carrera and take a Mediterranean cruise with the change. So why should you bother? What did the Lamborghini have that few other ultra-quick thoroughbreds did not? Exclusivity, that is what, with fewer than 300 Lamborghinis of all types in Britain at the time of our test. Its mean looking wedge shape and crisp, exciting V8 sound are what make most people turn their heads as you pass and draw inquisitive crowds wherever you stop. As an ego machine probably only half a dozen cars – including the Rolls-Royce Camargue – eclipse it. Yet in terms of sheer practicality the car has its short-comings, cramped 2+2 accommodation being only one. Nothing's perfect. A realistic approach helps.

You can count on your fingers the number of mid-engined sports cars made throughout the world. Most are 120 mph plus machines and several will top the magic 150. The Lamborghini Urraco P300 is among them, yet it is remarkably docile around town and refined enough when extended to make 150 mph feel more like 120.

Before the Urraco we had not rated those Lamborghinis we had driven as highly as their price tag and pedigree might suggest. The Urraco has its faults but in our experience (which does not yet include the Countach) it's the best Lamborghini yet to leave St Agata's palatial factory, perhaps in part because Lamborghini themselves now equip and trim the interior, leaving Bertone only to supply the painted shells.

The Urraco first appeared in 1972 as a striking but cramped 2+2 with a 220 bhp (DIN) 2·5-litre V8 installed transversely behind the rear seats. It was unashamedly aimed at the Ferrari Dino and Porsche buyer, but in its original form, truly sparkling performance was lacking. A further 500 cc and an extra 30 bhp has altered that, for the 3-litre Urraco is only marginally slower than the 4·7-litre Maserati Bora with a rev-limited maximum speed of 158 mph.

If 7·6 sec from rest to 60 mph does not compare *that* favourably with the opposition (notably the Porsche Carrera at 5·5 sec) then it is in part because of two factors: a soft clutch which necessitated gentle starts, and the slow gearchange from first to second. Even so, the acceleration will certainly keep your neck muscles in trim.

The noise from the four tail pipes may be music to an enthusiast's ear, but the law may regard it as anti-social, if not illegal. At mid-range speeds it produces a pleasant, burbling noise; raise the revs and the drainpipe exhausts emit a deep, guttural bark which changes to a typical twin ohc scream when the marvellous V8 is extended. The engine revs quickly and freely, the power coming in very strongly from below 2000 rpm and still going strong at the red-lined 7500 rpm. There is a cut-out at 8000 rpm.

Even more impressive is the engine's flexibility. You can trickle down to walking pace in 5th gear and pull away without complaint provided the throttle is fed in gently; too heavy a right boot and the four Weber carburettors simply drown the flame. We recorded 9·1 sec from 30-50 mph in 5th, a task the Carrera refused to perform, while the same increment in 4th was covered in a vigorous 5·3 sec.

Fuel economy is not good but we did drive the car hard. It returned 13·6 mpg overall on 100 octane fuel although one quick 200-mile cross-country journey using the engine's excellent flexibility to the full (rather than screaming through the gears), returned practically 16 mpg, giving a maximum range of 280 miles on the car's 17·6 gallon tank. We were not able to check steady speed fuel consumption.

The gate for the five-speed gearbox is biased – with first down to the left opposite reverse – towards a left-hand drive seating position. This, coupled with long and heavy lever movements makes the change very demanding at first. Drivers only warmed to it once they had discovered the knack of taking up the slack first, then being quick, sharp and very firm. The clutch is quite heavy and its long pedal travel has to be used to the full for clean disengagement. Its action is smooth, though, and the drive is well cushioned.

First gear is a little high (at 47 mph maximum) but the other ratios are fine, with second good for 65, third for 91·5, fourth for 125 and fifth, which will pull 7 500 rpm, 158 mph. The gearbox was quiet except for a whine when cold.

With a mid-engined configuration giving a front/rear weight bias of 41/59 per cent you would expect the car to handle well. It does when compared with any ordinary car. But the steering is fairly low geared and lacks the instant response of a Porsche's. The car also understeers too much and the slightly under-damped front is caught out by mid-corner bumps which send the nose hopping outwards. It should be much more neutral. Even so the cornering powers on its huge Michelin XWX radial tyres are very high and the car is superbly stable at speed.

The brakes are also outstanding. The pedal is firm as the action of the twin-circuit four ventilated discs is progressive and their

stopping power excellent. Only round MIRA's road circuit where we repeatedly pulled the car down from 120 mph for a succession of slow corners did they show any trace of fade. On the road they inspire confidence though. The handbrake would not hold the car on even slight slopes.

Rear seat space in most mid-engined 2 + 2s is poor but the Urraco is worse than most since there is not a lot of room up front either and headroom is limited. With some space sharing a small third person can be accommodated sitting sideways in the back but the compromise is not comfortable. We packed a reasonable 5·6 cu ft of test luggage in the boot but the compartment is above the exhaust pipes and contents get very warm!

Apart from what feels like inadequate damping on undulating roads, which makes the front bounce, the ride is very good – as it has been on every Lamborghini we have driven. The car barely rolls when cornered hard and generally is very comfortable with none of the suspension noise normally associated with small high performance cars.

Although the driving position is the most comfortable of any Lamborghini we have

tried, it is still not very good. If the steering wheel is within easy reach then your legs are cramped; if the pedals are right then the wheel is too far away. However, Lamborghini say that the position can be tailored to individual requirements, so include your vital statistics with the cheque.

The pedals were too close so it was possible to accelerate and brake simul-taneously if you were not careful. These deficiencies, together with a narrow seat and flat cushion and a static seat belt which cut across your neck, made the driving position tiring on long journeys.

Instrumentation is lavish and legible al-though the speedometer (reading to 180 mph) and rev counter (red-lined at 7500 rpm) are set far apart at each end of the wide facia binnacle. Those gauges essential for long-distance high-speed work (oil pressure, temperature, water and fuel) are directly ahead, as if to emphasise that the Urraco is designed more for the pleasures of the unrestricted open road than speed-limited countries.

Visibility is reasonable provided you remember the sloping nose and hidden tail when parking. Although you sit very low in the car the waistline is shallow so forward and side visibility is good. The rear view would be better if the slats covering the engine bay were edge-on to the driver's line of vision.

Quick action halogen headlamps pop up from beneath bonnet shrouds when you trip a facia switch. They give a wide spread of white light but lack sufficient penetration for really quick nocturnal driving. The two auxiliary lamps are for signalling other drivers only.

A refrigeration unit is standard, and it was most welcome during the Riviera-type weather of our test, especially as the sharply raked front screen has a glass-house effect on the interior. Cheesecutter ventilation grilles direct an icy blast through 180 degrees but it is not possible to get a cold flow directly to the face. It was not cold enough to test the heating properly.

Only when it is revved hard does noise from the engine become obtrusive, though the guttural exhaust bark and mechanical clatter at speed may sound pleasant to some. At 80-90 mph the car feels and sounds very relaxed. Wind noise is exceptionally low, and the transmission only whines when cold.

The interior is very smart. The facia is trimmed in suede and natural leather adorns the doors and edges of the seats which have cloth inserts. The high quality close-pile carpet is colour keyed, as is the padded roof lining. Although stereo speakers and a roof-mounted aerial are included in the package, a radio is not. There is no heated rear window either, but the proximity of the engine to the back light makes one unnecessary. The side windows are electrically operated and, like the car, move quickly.

The Urraco is well made. The doors close with a satisfying 'clunk. and the coachwork is excellent. Now that Lamborghini are responsible for interior trim the standard is high, with everything fitting as it should. Perfectionists might quibble about there being no caps over the screw heads inside the passenger compartment, but that is about all.

Having seen how development machines are thrashed over the old Mille Miglia course, subjecting them to far higher stresses than we imposed on our car, we are satisfied that The Incident which seems to be a fateful part of any association we have with

a Lamborghini, was another of those one-off freaks. The failure of a fabricated bracket locating the left-hand rear strut (the possible consequences of which do not need elaborating) caused such despondency at the concessionaires that the offending component was immediately returned to the factory for analysis. None of the other 600 Urracos so far made have apparently suffered such a failure.

Otherwise, everyone on *Motor* enjoyed the P300 more than they expected, and voted it the best Lamborghini yet.

As mentioned on page 17, the Lamborghini company is being held in a mild form of receivership following their failure to meet the commitment with BMW to build the bodies for the German company's mid-engined M1. The Urraco P300 (and P250) were still listed, not significantly changed since *Motor*'s 1975 road test.

GENERAL SPECIFICATION

Engine

Cylinders	8 in vee, mid-mounted
Capacity	2 997 cc
Bore/stroke	86 × 64·5 mm
Cooling	water
Block	alloy
Head	alloy
Valves	dohc per bank
Compression	10·4:1
Carburettor	4 Weber 40DCNF
Bearings	5 main
Max power	250 bhp (DIN) at 7 500 rpm
Max torque	166 lb-ft (DIN) at 5 750 rpm

Transmission

Type	5-speed manual
Internal ratios and mph/1000 rpm	
Top	0·870:1/21·1
4th	1·185:1/16·7
3rd	1·565:1/12·2
2nd	2·105:1/8·7
1st	2·933:1/6·3
Rev	2·856:1
Final drive	4·0:1

Body/Chassis

Construction	unitary, steel

Suspension

Front	independent by MacPherson struts
Rear	independent by MacPherson struts, anti-roll bar

Steering

Type	rack and pinion
Assistance	no

Brakes

Front	discs
Rear	discs
Servo	yes
Circuit	split

Wheels/Tyres

Type	7½J × 14 in
Tyres	195/70 VR14 (front); 205/70 VR14 (rear)

Electrical

Battery	12v, 55 a-h
Earth	negative
Generator	55 amp alternator
Fuses	12
Headlights	2 halogen

PERFORMANCE DATA

Maximum speeds				*mph*	*rpm*
Top	...	...	...	158	7 500
4th	...	...	...	125	7 500
3rd	...	...	...	92	7 500
2nd	...	...	...	65	7 500
1st	...	...	...	47	7 500

Acceleration from rest				
mph				*sec*
0-30	...	...	...	3·0
0-40	...	...	...	4·0
0-50	...	...	...	5·8
0-60	...	...	...	7·6
0-70	...	...	...	9·8
0-80	...	...	...	11·6
0-90	...	...	...	14·0
0-100	...	...	...	17·5
0-110	...	...	...	20·8
0-120	...	...	...	25·3
Standing ¼ mile	...	...		15·6
Standing km	...	...		27·8

Acceleration in		5th	4th
mph		*sec*	*sec*
20-40	...	9·6	5·9
30-50	...	9·1	5·3
40-60	...	9·1	4·8
50-70	...	8·2	4·7
60-80	...	7·0	5·5
70-90	...	7·1	5·2
80-100	...	8·3	5·4
90-110	...	9·8	5·6
100-120	...	11·1	—

Fuel consumption

Touring (estimated)*	16 mpg
Overall	13·6 mpg
Tank capacity	17·6 gal
Max range	280 miles

*Consumption midway between 30 mph and maximum speed less 5% allowance for acceleration. Maximum range is based on touring consumption.

FERRARI 365GT4BB

For Italians the name of Ferrari is almost commonplace (their telephone books abound with it), while the rest of the world associates it with just one man, Enzo, and his apparently never-ending stream of all-conquering racing and breath-taking road cars. The magic of this famous marque stretches to all corners of the globe and is arguably stronger than that of any other current make. With Niki Lauda's recent Championship successes in Formula 1 in a Ferrari we have again been reminded of the skill and craftsmanship of this firm. Gracefully styled, neck-twinging cars like the Boxer are further roadgoing proof.

The Boxer is the first 'full sized' Ferrari to enjoy a mid-engined configuration, and shares many features of its stablemates, past and present. Like its predecessor, the front-engined Daytona, it is an uncompromising mile-eater for two, and only two. Luggage accommodation is minimal, in fact inferior to that of the Daytona. Also, like the Daytona, it is powered by a four-cam, 12-cylinder engine although in this case the cams are belt driven rather than chain driven and the cylinders horizontally opposed (hence the Boxer nomenclature) rather than in the more normal Ferrari road configuration of a 60 degree V.

Far from being a detuned version of their successful flat-12 Formula 1 engine, however, the Boxer's unit can be considered more as a flattened V12, the connecting rods of opposing pistons sharing common crank pins. These rods and several other components are interchangeable with those in the 'V' engines of the same capacity.

As in the transverse-engined Dino models, the Boxer's five-speed gearbox and transaxle are housed below the engine. Again like the Dino, the Boxer has a body chassis unit of mixed construction, a square-tube perimeter frame strengthened with sheet steel and capped with mainly aluminium alloy panels. The fore and aft sections of the lower body are, however, made of glass-fibre.

Few people will ever enjoy the opportunity of stepping over the Boxer's deep sills and snuggling into the beautifully functional cockpit, let alone sampling the exciting performance first hand. Each Boxer costs more than many people will ever spend on homes let alone cars. What, then, has driven the owners to part with so much for what is, after all is said and done, just another means of transport?

Just a view of the engine alone is sufficient to set many a mouth watering, and goes some way to explaining the price tag too. Nestling under a pair of long flat intakes are no fewer than four triple-choke Webers. The 12 sparking plugs are all clearly visible as is the double-deck Marelli distributor that feeds them. Despite an identical capacity of 4390 cc the power of the Boxer is even greater than that of its predecessor; 380 bhp (DIN) as opposed to the 352 claimed for the Daytona. It also has a smaller, lighter shell of apparently clean, very aerodynamic lines. Small wonder, then, that the figure of 200 mph has been suggested as a potential maximum speed for the BB. Ferrari themselves claim 188 mph while the Italian government have the car 'homologated' at a mean speed of 171 mph. Sadly we are not in a position to confirm these figures as there is no longer any place where it would be

legally and socially acceptable to complete a series of accurate maximum speed tests. We did experience speeds of 150 mph on several occasions, however, at which point the car was still accelerating hard and we have little doubt that something in excess of 170 mph would have shown before long had the track been long enough. Certainly, like its predecessor it is at speeds above 100 mph that the Boxer impresses most, although to be fair to the Daytona the mid-engined car did not actually show any evidence of those supposed extra horses.

While equally thrilling, accelerating a Boxer is a very different pastime from putting a Daytona through its paces. With a good proportion (including the flywheel) of the engine overhanging the axle centre-line it is perhaps not surprising that some 56 per cent of the car's 3420 lb rests on the rear tyres. So despite all the power, high revs are needed before traction can be broken. On MIRA's grippy surface some 4000 rpm were required to assure progressive wheelspin rather than the offending clutchslip that resulted from too few revs. Rubber-burning starts were also the only ones that ensured you remained within the power band, which effectively runs from 4000 rpm to the red line at 7700 rpm.

Unfortunately Mr Pininfarina made no provision for fitting fifth wheels when he designed the Boxer's tail, and as time was short we had no option but to take our speed readings off the car's own electronic speedometer, following careful recalibration. Add to this the usual problems of a dog-leg gearchange occurring just before 60 mph, and the previously experienced (and heart-stopping) tendency for Ferrari clutches to go over centre on fast changes, and it is perhaps surprising we achieved the figures we did. Even so, they do not match the factory's claims. From rest to 60 mph took 6·5 sec, and we rocketed past the 100 mph mark in a mean of 13·5 sec. Supercar times by any standards, but not quite in the Daytona league.

In many ways the top gear figures were more impressive, especially around the 100 mph region; 80-100 for instance, took a disdainful 5·8 sec. That is a shatteringly short time for a car capable of such a high terminal speed and one that clearly demonstrates the considerable torque of the flat-12 engine.

Starting was straightforward, a few pumps on the long travel accelerator being sufficient to prime the engine, although occasionally a second round of pumping was needed before all twelve cylinders would come cleanly on song. The engine then pulled without further fuss. Sudden depression of the accelerator below 3000 rpm could result in an irritating hesitation, and you soon learn to ease the throttle when in this range. From there on the flow of power was smooth and very satisfying all the way up

to, and even beyond the red line if you were not wary. The mechanical gnashings of the 'flat' engine are noticeably less than those of the 'V' unit with its chain-driven cams. That marvellous Ferrari howl is still there, although arguably too loud.

Our 600-odd miles in the Boxer were composed of flat-out testing at MIRA and some rapid road driving, which resulted in an overall consumption of 11·1 mpg on 100 octane fuel. More miles and more normal driving to compensate for the testing would doubtless have improved the figure. Yet more light-footed treatment could have resulted in around 15 mpg and a range of almost 400 miles from the 26·4-gallon tank, but we doubt if many owners would drive as gently as that.

Like the neat Momo leather rimmed steering wheel, the five-speed, gated gearbox and its longish lever are typical Ferrari features. The box itself is an all-indirect, two-shaft, constant-mesh unit with Porsche-type synchromesh which in turn drives through a ZF limited slip differential.

Ferrari gearboxes can be difficult at first but invariably then respond to well-timed changes; the Boxer's was no exception. With the oil properly warmed, the lever would clonk satisfyingly from slot to slot provided the clutch was pressed well down, whereas poorly matched revs or a tiring clutch foot (the pedal is very heavy) usually resulted in some baulking. It needed concentration to make consistently clean changes too, for despite its long travel the accelerator delivered all 380 bhp pretty briskly. Reverse was always difficult to engage.

Understandably the steering of the Boxer is far more akin to that of the Dino's than previous 'big' Ferraris. The Daytona's was very heavy and a bit dead, that of the Boxer is well weighted and endowed with ordinary feel as well as that imparted by the traditional

speeds far higher than one would normally be exploring on public roads, the leech-like grip of the Michelin XWX tyres being quite sufficient to allow a relatively neutral and totally undramatic progress at a more law-abiding pace. Ground clearance was a problem, as the exhaust system made contact on numerous occasions during one of our more spirited drives.

The specification of the ATE brakes is impressive, consisting of four-pot calipers operating ventilated discs front and rear through twin hydraulic circuits. We found the offset pedal full of feel and reassuringly powerful even when arresting all 3420 lb from speeds over 150 mph. Repeating the procedure however was not so easy, their effectiveness tailing-off noticeably with each application. Recovery from the fade was almost instantaneous, however.

A tug on an under-facia lever releases both catches of the front-hinged nose section and reveals what little luggage space there is. Much of this area is occupied by the space-saver spare tyre (limited to 90 mph) leaving room for little more than the proverbial toothbrush and comb. More case space is found behind the seats, although its volume depends on the seat positions. Smaller oddments can be stowed in the door pockets, in the glovebox and in the bin to the right.

Ferrari kickback. The handling was untypical of a mid-engined car in that increasing throttle on a fast bend resulted in a reduction rather than an increase in understeer. This made the car delightfully responsive for rapid negotiation of smooth roads. Really fast driving on more bumpy surfaces, however, would sometimes cause the tail to let go completely, calling for very rapid correction. However, we are now talking of

Headroom is just about sufficient for most drivers, although as far as we could see the driving position was little more adaptable than that of the Daytona. The pedals were fixed and there was no tilt facility on the leather covered bucket seats, but the backrests were reclining. The ride, although suitably taut, was far from uncomfortable and only the severest of minor road bumps caused the suspension to run out of travel. Even then there was little more than a distant thud from the car's commendably stiff structure.

The cockpit has a typically functional layout, with all major and minor controls neatly labelled and within easy reach of the driving seat. Lights, indicators and the wash/wipe control for the single parallelogram wiper are all stalk operated from the column.

A mass of switches decorates the console too. Most look after the disappointing air conditioning system, which has no face-level vents and directs most of its air straight over the occupants' heads. The remaining knobs control the hazard flashers and electric windows. Ahead of the driver are a bevy of boldy calibrated instruments which for night use have a subtle red glow illuminating their red numerals. Seat belts are always a problem on a car of this type and the installation of the Boxer's static ones were about as good as you could expect. Had they been easily adjustable they would not have fallen off the shoulder. Adjustment, however, was particularly awkward and they did.

In these stratospheric price regions you have a right to expect quality workmanship. In most respects we were impressed by Scaglietti's executions of this striking Pininfarina design. The doors clicked shut and the nose and tail sections were precision made. The fit of the facia was indifferent though, and as with the 308 Dino, the door trim and hidden releases smacked of cost savings out of character in this class of car.

The view from the driving seat is off-putting at first. The graceful bonnet curves away out of sight and as in all mid-engined designs, rear three-quarter vision is very limited. Lateral and rearward views are adequate though. The single wiper and slave blade make a reasonable job of cleaning the car's steeply canted windscreen and the halogen lights are extremely powerful on main beam if only average when dipped. One final drawback of the layout is the reflections that come from the rear vertical screen, particularly at night.

While the Boxer breaks new ground for Ferrari it is no trend-setter in the idiom of the 246 GT or other Ferrari classics like the 275 GTB4, arguably the greatest of them all. Its performance is not mind-bending or perhaps even quite as brutish as the Daytona's although it is sufficient to place it firmly in the supercar class. The handling does not compare with say the smaller, nimbler 246 GT but it is still pretty impressive for a car of this size and weight. The brake fade was less acceptable. Over less excusable, more niggling details like the inefficient air conditioning and the lack of luggage space we must not dwell too long. Merely remember it is a Ferrari and that alone explains why some owners each parted with the price of a good size house in order to own a Boxer.

A year after this autumn 1975 road test, the Ferrari Boxer gained a new 5-litre version of the flat 12 engine, developing 360 bhp. The body was extended by $2\frac{1}{2}$ in in length to accommodate it, and the wheel arches flared to accommodate fatter tyres. Other changes included a front spoiler and NACA ducts to admit cool air at the rear.

GENERAL SPECIFICATION

Engine

Cylinders	12 horizontally opposed
Capacity	4 391 cc
Bore/stroke	81 × 71 mm
Cooling	water
Block	alloy
Head	alloy
Valves	dohc per bank
Compression	8·8:1
Carburettor	4 Weber 40IF3C triple-choke
Bearings	7 main
Max power	380 (DIN) at 7 200 rpm
Max torque	302 lb-ft (DIN) at 3 900 rpm

Transmission

Type	5-speed manual
Internal ratios and mph/1000 rpm	
Top	0·821:1/25·4
4th	1·080:1/19·3
3rd	1·428:1/14·6
2nd	1·888:1/11·1
1st	2·642:1/7·9
Rev	2·357:1
Final drive	3·75:1

Body/Chassis

Construction	tubular steel frame with steel, alloy and glassfibre panels

Suspension

Front	independent by double wishbones, coil springs, anti-roll bar
Rear	independent by double wishbones, twin coils, anti-roll bar

Steering

Type	rack and pinion
Assistance	no

Brakes

Front	11·3 in ventilated discs
Rear	11·7 in ventilated discs
Servo	yes
Circuit	twin independent

Wheels/Tyres

Type	alloy, $7\frac{1}{2}$J × 15 in
Tyres	215/70 VR15 Michelin XWX

Electrical

Battery	12v, 74 a-h
Earth	negative
Generator	alternator
Fuses	20
Headlights	four quartz halogen

PERFORMANCE DATA

Maximum speeds

	mph	rpm
Top	170+	—
4th	135	7000
3rd	102	7000
2nd	78	7000
1st	55	7000

Acceleration from rest

mph	sec
0-50	4·8
0-60	6·5
0-70	8·4
0-80	10·1
0-90	11·8
0-100...	13·5
0-110...	16·7
0-120...	19·7

Acceleration in top

mph	sec
50-70	7·6
60-80	7·5
70-90	6·8
80-100	5·8
90-110	6·6
100-120	8·2

Fuel consumption

Touring (estimated)*	15 mpg
Overall	11·1 mpg
Tank capacity	26·4 gal
Max range	396 miles

*Consumption midway between 30 mph and maximum speed less 5% allowance for acceleration.
Maximum range is based on touring consumption.

PORSCHE 3.0 Turbo

Porsche have won just about everything worth winning in motor sport. In the late 1960s, when rallying was probably at its most competitive, they dominated the world scene and won numerous international events. They have had the upper hand in motor racing for even longer, and their successes have included Le Mans, Can Am, the World Championship of Makes.

All history of course. What you may have overlooked is that Porsche's basic competition weapon (prototypes excepted) *since 1966* has been the 911. And it still wins. Look at the results of any sports car race or international rally, and the chances are that a very high proportion of the top finishers will be in 911s.

To remain competitive for such a long time, Porsche have continually developed the 911, resisting change for the sake of it, but sticking to the same basic engineering: a flat-six overhung at the rear, MacPherson strut suspension at the front and semi-trailing arms at the rear, and springing by torsion bars. Almost every advance in the design of the racing cars has been paralleled, where applicable, by a similar improvement to the road cars. Tangible evidence that racing can improve the breed.

It is no surprise, therefore, that the two 911 variants that represent the culmination of the racing and road development programmes are very similar in concept. The racer, called the Carrera Turbo, came 2nd at Le Mans in 1975 and had a 2·1 litre turbocharged engine producing 450 bhp at 8000 rpm. It shares many parts with Porsche's road-going flagship (called simply the Turbo) which has a 3·0 litre turbocharged engine, producing a more modest 260 bhp at 5500 rpm. With its shapely, extended wheel arches, enormous low-profile Pirelli tyres, as well as the workmanlike spoilers front and rear, the Turbo's racing ancestry is very obvious.

But do not be misled. The Turbo is not a noisy, unrefined racer-turned-road-car. Far from it. It is probably the most civilised Porsche yet – and easily the best. Not one of the Porsche's rivals (and considering the Turbo's price tag, we are talking of the most expensive, most exotic Supercars in the world) is pleasant to drive in heavy traffic; the Porsche is. Not one of the Porsche's rivals is quiet enough to be driven in comfort on long journeys; the Porsche is.

The admirable thing about the Turbo is that this refinement has not been achieved by sacrificing what Porsche owners cherish most: driver appeal. The straight-line performance is shattering, the winding road performance even more so, where the incredible braking, road-holding and traction can be used to full advantage. We doubt that there is any car in the world that is faster along a twisting road; there certainly is not a car that gives any more satisfaction when driven well. We have always admired Porsche for producing beautifully engineered machines. In the Turbo, they have the finest driving machine you can buy.

The body style and aerodynamic paraphernalia of the Turbo are the same as those of the Carrera RS 3·0 (the homologation 'special' from which the full race RSR was developed). The rear suspension incorporates the modified pick-up points used on later RS models that were designed to keep the outer rear wheel more upright during hard cornering. The rear torsion bars are stiffer than those of the normal 911s (as are the anti-roll bars at both ends), and at the front, anti-dive has been increased to the amount used on the racing Turbo. To cope with the extra torque, the rear wheel bearing is of a stiffer type, first used on the 917.

One of the racing Turbo's weakest points was its transmission. Although the existing five-speed gearbox could easily cope with the power and torque output of the road-going turbocharged 3·0 litre engine, it did not have enough strength in reserve for a racing version. Porsche therefore developed a special four-speed gearbox with wider gears and a larger clutch (approximately 9·5 in diameter).

The turbocharger (which is a centrifugal supercharger driven by a turbine in the engine's exhaust system) is made by KKK and is controlled by a sophisticated waste-gate system. When the correct boost pressure is reached (0·8 atm, about 12 psi) exhaust gases are diverted from the turbocharger's turbine to keep that pressure constant. Should this system go wrong, or there be a combustion blow back, Porsche fit a fail-safe blow-off valve on the inlet manifold.

A Bosch K-Jetronic fuel injection system supplies the fuel, while Bosch also make the fully electronic contactless ignition system.

The compression ratio is very low at 6·5:1; but this is made up by the fixed induction which the turbocharger provides. The maximum power of 260 bhp (DIN) is produced at 5500 rpm which makes an interesting comparison with the normally aspirated 2·7 litre Carrera's figures of 210 bhp at 6300 rpm. What is even more impressive is the large spread of power that the engine gives; between 4000 and 6500 rpm you have over 200 bhp on tap, and over 4800 rpm, there is at least 240 bhp. Maximum torque is quoted as 253 lb ft at 4000 rpm.

Like other turbocharged engines, the Turbo has a very distinct power band. At low rpm, it does not cough or splutter like a highly tuned conventional engine of the same specific power output might; it pulls, but not particularly strongly, and certainly with no hint of the shattering performance higher up the rev range.

We do not know of any other 150 mph car that will take full throttle in top gear from a mere 750 rpm (20 mph). From 20 to 40 mph in this gear takes 9·9 sec, from 30 to 50 mph only 9·6 sec. This is one of the most impressive features of the Turbo.

Even so, like every Porsche that has gone before, the Turbo thrives on revs. The turbocharger starts augmenting the car's power output at about 3800-4000 rpm (you cannot tell precisely as Porsche do not provide a boost gauge). The result is a neck-snapping surge of acceleration that presses you hard back into the seat no matter what gear you are in. It is not jerky or particularly vicious, more the sort of surge that you get when a jet releases its brakes on take-off.

The lag in response when lifting the throttle (giving a running-away feeling) we noticed when driving a prototype earlier this year was absent on this car. Any lag on opening the throttle from a partially or fully closed position (for instance when changing gear) is barely noticeable and not as pronounced as that of other turbocharged engines. The only characteristic you must become accustomed to is the sudden surge of power as the turbocharger cuts in when accelerating from low revs. With acclimatisation you learn to anticipate it, and to moderate the throttle position accordingly.

Slingshot starts in a Porsche are rarely easy, as the grip afforded by wide tyres and the 911's tail-heavy weight distribution normally defeated all attempts to spin the wheels. One exception to this was the last Carrera (2·7 litre) we tested with which beautifully controlled wheelspin starts, even on MIRA's grippy surface, were possible.

The grip given by the Turbo's extra-wide rear tyres more than offsets its extra power

(260 bhp instead of 210). No matter how vicious you are with the clutch, or how many revs you use, it's only possible to spin the rear wheels for a couple of feet. As the tyres grip, the engine speed drops below that necessary for the turbocharger to operate, resulting in initial acceleration less startling than we had anticipated. Incidentally, we did try much more gentle, clutch-slip starts but the times were about the same.

To reach 60 mph from rest took 6·0 sec (the Carrera took only 5·5 sec); 80 mph came up in 8·5 sec (9·4 sec for the Carrera) and 100 mph in 13·2 sec (14·9 sec for the Carrera). Over 100 mph the Turbo's superior power and better aerodynamics start to count. The Turbo reaches 120 mph in 19·3 sec (compared to the Carrera's 23·4 sec). The top gear times are even more revealing for despite the Turbo's long legged gait of 26·2 mph/1000 rpm in fourth (the Carrera's fifth gives 23·3 mph/1000 rpm), from 90 to 110 mph takes only 7·4 sec against 11·3 sec of the Carrera.

Although we had no opportunity to verify Porsche's claim of over 155 mph maximum speed, we achieved true speeds of over 145 mph easily within the limited confines of MIRA on a number of occasions. It seems likely that Porsche's assertion is, if anything, a little conservative.

One by-product of the turbocharger's complex inlet and exhaust plumbing is that the engine is quieter than that of other Porsches and very much quieter than other exotic cars. Little of the normal exhaust rasp and cam drive scream reach the interior – a pleasing or disappointing feature depending on your point of view. Even when driven very hard the Turbo does not become obtrusively noisy, and the car can be driven for extended periods without engine noise becoming tiresome.

Considering the car's performance, the fuel consumption of 15·0 mpg obtained for our 600-mile test is excellent, and would probably have been even better over a greater mileage to offset a high proportion of

hard road driving and all-out performance testing at MIRA. Porsche's claim of 18 mpg does not sound unrealistic. The 17·6 gallon tank would give a range of just over 300 miles at this consumption.

Porsche consider four gearbox ratios to be sufficient for the Turbo, in view of its good low speed torque. We disagree. The maximum speeds in each of the intermediate gears at 6700 rpm is 51, 88 and 129 mph. For slow, tight corners there is not an ideal gear; first is too low and fierce, second is too high and the engine drops out of the power band. Fourth could be even higher, too. At 155 mph the engine is well past its power peak, so that apart from making the car a little more economical and even more relaxed at speed, a higher cruising ratio might make it faster too. We would like to see five, more closely spaced, ratios.

The gearchange itself is pure Porsche. The lever has fairly long movements and does not feel particularly precise, but the change is fast, light and baulk-free. The clutch has a slight over-centre action but is light and progressive.

With the Turbo, Porsche must have laid the myth that rear engined cars do not handle to rest for ever. The biggest difference between this version of the 911 and its predecessors is the adoption of wide ultra-low profile Pirelli tyres of racing ancestry. These tyres endow the Turbo with unbelievable cornering powers. The car will corner without drama at speeds that only a few years ago would have been regarded as impossible. The reserves of adhesion are so great that as far as road driving is concerned, to talk about oversteer and under-

steer is meaningless. The Turbo simply steers.

Lifting the throttle in mid-corner does cause the nose to tuck-in slightly but never is this tendency great enough to call for more than a small steering correction. Only once in the whole of our test did the tail step out of line, when the car was accelerated hard in first gear out of a slow, adverse camber corner. A quick application of opposite lock was all that was required.

Complementing this excellent handling, the steering is near perfect: quick, accurate, light and responsive. There is less kickback than before; the gentle wriggling of the wheel in your hands over bumpy surfaces usefully increases the generous amount of feel that the steering gives. We were surprised how light the steering was when parking in view of the enormous tyres.

We cannot fault the brakes, either. The ATE ventilated discs feel reassuring and repeatedly pulled the Turbo down from high speeds without drama. No matter how hard we punished them they didn't fade – almost the reverse was true as the pedal got lighter as the linings warmed to their task.

The tyres also dominate the ride which feels harsh and unforgiving over small bumps and corrugations such as sunken manhole covers, although the noise transmitted through to the interior makes it sound a lot worse than it really is. At other times the ride is firm and well-controlled.

The excellent, well shaped seats are very comfortable and help to mask the ride's deficiencies and there is more than enough room for six footers to stretch their legs. Drivers should be able to tailor themselves an excellent driving position although some might find the gearlever and steering wheel a little far forward.

To cure the innate problem of varying temperature from the heater under different driving conditions, Porsche equip the Turbo with a thermostatically controlled heating system consisting of a temperature sensor mounted near the interior mirror and a servo motor which moves the heater temperature lever accordingly. We were not able to assess its effectiveness in the heatwave weather of our test, but it promises to be a solution to one of our persistent criticisms of Porsches – unstable heater output.

Our other perennial grouse – that there is no true fresh air ventilation – still applies. Opening the sunroof or windows (both electrically operated) helps but only at the expense of loud wind noise, and that is no real solution. The only option for Turbo owners is to have air conditioning.

As always, we liked the Porsche interior trim and finish. It is a delicate balance between functionality and plushness, and shows impeccable taste in the choice of materials – although Porsche stress that the type of interior trim is up to the customer – leather, leather/cloth inlays, etc.

Apart from being very fast and exciting, the Porsche is a practical car. Unlike most rivals which can only be regarded as Sunday morning adrenalin pumps because of their intractability, or cramped accommodation, the Turbo can be used as comfortable daily transport. Yet its handling and road-holding are probably as good as any other car in the world. Few cars have impressed us so much.

In mid-1977 Porsche enlarged the engine capacity of their flagship to 3·3 litres, increasing the maximum power to 300 bhp at 5 500 rpm and torque to a peak of 303 lb-ft at 4 000 rpm. The brakes and aerodynamic aids were improved to cope with the car's maximum claimed speed of 160 mph.

GENERAL SPECIFICATION

Engine

Cylinders	flat 6
Capacity	2 993 cc
Bore/stroke	95 × 70·4 mm
Cooling	air
Block	alloy
Head	alloy
Valves	sohc per bank
Compression	6·5:1
Fuel injection	Bosch K-Jetronic
Bearings	8 main
Max power	260 bhp (DIN) at 5 500 rpm
Max torque	253 lb-ft (DIN) at 4 000 rpm

Transmission

Type	4-speed manual	
Internal ratios and mph/1000 rpm		
Top	0·65:1/26·2	
4th	—	
3rd	0·89:1/19·2	
2nd	1·30:1/13·2	
1st	2·25:1/7·6	
Rev	2·43:1	
Final drive	4·00:1	

Body/Chassis

Construction	steel, unitary

Suspension

Front	independent by Macpherson strut, longitudinal torsion bars, anti-roll bar
Rear	independent by semi-trailing arms, transverse torsion bars, anti-roll bar

Steering

Type	rack and pinion
Assistance	no

Brakes

Front	ventilated discs
Rear	ventilated discs
Servo	no
Circuit	dual

Wheels/Tyres

Type	alloy, 7 × 15 in (front); 8 × 15 in (rear)
Tyres	Pirelli P7 205/50 VR15 (front); 225/50 VR15 (rear)

Electrical

Battery	12v, 66 a-h
Earth	negative
Generator	980 watt alternator
Fuses	24
Headlights	2 halogen

PERFORMANCE DATA

Maximum speeds		mph	rpm
Top (estimated)	...	155	—
3rd	... ...	129	6 700
2nd	... ...	88	6 700
1st	... ...	51	6 700

Acceleration from rest				
mph				sec
0-30	...	...	...	2·9
0-40	...	...	...	3·6
0-50	...	...	...	4·4
0-60	...	...	...	6·0
0-70	...	...	...	7·2
0-80	...	...	...	8·5
0-90	...	...	...	10·6
0-100	...	...	...	13·2
0-110	...	...	...	15·8
0-120	...	...	...	19·3
Standing ¼ mile	...	...	14·2	
Standing km.	...	...	25·6	

Acceleration in top				
mph				sec
10-30	...	...	...	—
20-40	...	...	...	9·9
30-50	...	...	...	9·6
40-60	...	...	...	9·7
50-70	...	...	...	9·4
60-80	...	...	...	8·3
70-90	...	...	...	6·1
80-100	...	...	...	6·3
90-110	...	...	...	7·4
100-120	...	...	...	8·8

Fuel consumption

Touring* (estimated)	18 mpg
Overall	15 mpg
Tank capacity	17·6 gal
Max range	317 miles

*Consumption between 30 mph and maximum speed less 5% allowance for acceleration. Maximum range is based on touring consumption.

LAMBORGHINI Countach

Many styling exercises produced for motor shows are impractical, exaggerated machines never intended for production. They are often commissioned for prestige and publicity reasons by large firms to demonstrate the talents of young designers and to see just what can be done when normal constraints are thrown to the wind. If you cannot change a plug without removing the engine first or even see out properly because of internal reflections, it is of little consequence.

Surprisingly, a number of these so-called one-offs *do* get into production. The Lotus Esprit is one, Lamborghini's most exotic and expensive creation yet, the Countach, is another.

Few people gazing at the original Bertone Countach at Geneva in 1971 could have regarded it as anything other than a 'show' car. There were those fold-up doors for a start (how did you get out if the car rolled?) and the space-age cockpit with its abysmal rear visibility, not to mention the strange engine/transmission configuration.

Bertone and Lamborghini had mounted the all-alloy V12 engine longitudinally in the chassis (abandoning the Miura's transverse layout), but with the gearbox at its front in the centre of the car. The drive was taken from the gearbox's secondary shaft by a drop-gear to a propeller shaft running rearwards to the final drive housed in an extension of the cast-alloy sump. The intention was to give better weight distribution and a more positive gearchange than the Miura had, which sounded reasonable enough; but would Lamborghini be able to make this unconventional arrangement work well enough on a production car. It seemed unlikely.

Yet intended for production the Countach (pronounced 'coontash', incidentally) certainly was. Two years were spent testing and developing the design (most effort being put into perfecting the unorthodox power train) and when non-prototype versions appeared at the end of 1973 only a pair of NACA ducts on the car's flanks and a couple of radiator cowls on its haunches betrayed externally the many mechanical changes under the skin.

The original cobbled-up semi-monocoque chassis had been replaced by a more conventional (and very much more complex) tubular spaceframe; the ingenious periscope mirror arrangement had been dropped in favour of a more conventional mirror;

and the larger 4·8 litre engine was shelved indefinitely. Announced as the world's most expensive and fastest production car, as well as being the replacement for the legendary Miura, the Countach had a lot to live up to.

Lamborghini only make one a week, so it is certainly exclusive. But there are better reasons than that for buying a Countach. True, it is rare and it does have the style, panache and rakish lines that attract fascinated attention. But it is also an extremely well engineered car and perhaps deserves more respect than bestowed on a rich man's toy. Shattering performance allied to excellent handling, roadholding and brakes add up to a formidable package, as well they ought for the price!

For the Countach, the Lamborghini four overhead camshaft V12 engine of 3929 cc differs only in details from the unit that used to power the Miura. The special cast Elektron sump incorporating the differential housing is one obvious change, as are the double rows of horizontal Weber 45DCOE carburettors (six in all) that dominate the engine – the Miura had four triple down-draught carburettors. The engine produces 375 bhp (DIN) at 8000 rpm – not much under 100 bhp/litre, a yardstick by which people used to judge full-blooded racing engines not so long ago. Times have changed!

Not surprisingly, the engine thrives on revs. There is little point in using less than 4000 rpm for anything other than gentle cruising on a whiff of throttle; open the throttle suddenly at low rpm and the engine cuts dead. But above 4000 rpm it is another story. The exhaust note deepens perceptibly as the car gathers speed and the engine gets a new lease of life as it passes 6000 rpm, when it develops the characteristic V12 – almost F1-like – scream. The way in which it surges on towards the 8000 rpm red line is most exhilarating, especially as there is no detectable fall-off in power.

We had to do our performance tests on a brand-new, barely run-in example. This perhaps explains why the engine felt rougher and more inflexible than those of other Lamborghinis we have tried.

Even so, the acceleration was startling. On MIRA's grippy horizontal straight, doing a racing-style start was not easy, for the clutch lacked bite and slipped if the revs dropped. The only solution was to suppress our feelings of mechanical sympathy, wind the motor up to 7000 rpm (perilously close to the limit) and release the clutch as quickly and as sharply as possible. The results, were spectacular. Plumes of tyre smoke, a raucous bellow from the exhausts, a neck-jerking surge of acceleration, black lines 50 yards long (we measured them!) and a 0-60 mph time of 5·6 sec. The first to second gearchange came at 65 mph, the next at 83 mph and after only 13·1 sec from rest the car was

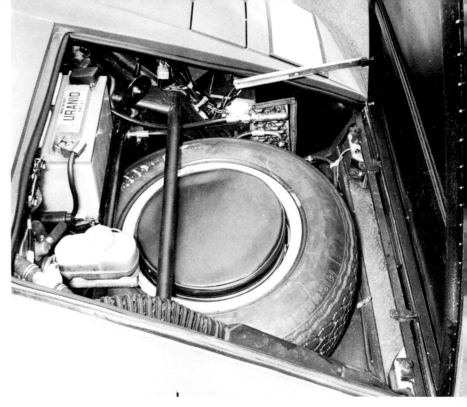

doing 100 mph. The quarter mile mark rushed past a fraction later (14·1 sec).

Fast by any standards, but Lamborghini say that a well run-in example should be even quicker.

Lamborghini also claim a top speed of over 190 mph, but needless to say we did not find a road where we could safely (or legally) confirm the figure. Our car seemed to be struggling at 160 mph – we suspect the new engine was not properly on song – and we would estimate its top speed to be around 175 mph.

At first sight the enormous fuel tanks (mounted racing-style either side of the passenger compartment and *each* with a capacity of 13·2 gallons) appear more than adequate. But our Countach only did 10 mpg so we could only travel just over 250 miles between stops. Filling the tanks is not easy either, for the caps are hidden beneath well-camouflaged flaps inside the NACA ducts on each side of the car: a pump attendant's nightmare.

With the gearbox much closer to the driver than in many conventional mid-engined cars, the lever linkage is shorter and the gearchange benefits considerably from the greater precision that this gives. Like all other Lamborghinis (and Ferraris), the five-speed gear pattern is arranged with first across to the left and back, and there is an external metal gate to guide the lever. Both these features are a little off-putting to start with; first to second is an awkward dog-leg and the metal gate enforces accurate movements of the lever. But with a little acclimatisation (and miles – our car's change freed up noticeably during the test) it becomes quite manageable. It is not a sophisticated gearchange though – it is much too heavy for that – but it *is* fast and the synchromesh unbeatable. Straight-through changes bring forth some groans and shrieks from the gearbox, however.

Gearbox and transmission noise are loud and disturbing. At high rpm – particularly in third gear – the gearlever chatters, zizzes and transmits far too much whine through to the interior. Covering the open gate with your hand reduces the noise, suggesting that some simple soundproofing would be beneficial.

Apart from the low second gear, the gearbox ratios are well chosen. Maxima in

the intermediate gears at 8000 rpm are 65, 83, 115 and 149 mph. Fifth gives the car a long legged gait of 23.7 mph/1000 rpm, although a slightly lower final drive might be an improvement for the car feels over-geared and relatively sluggish in top, an impression exaggerated by the car's poor flexibility.

From the F1-type Koni dampers to the suspension arms and links, the suspension and steering are fully adjustable, which means that, within limits, you can set up a Countach to handle and ride as you wish. The factory normally adjusts the cars so that they handle as near neutrally as possible. Our car had its front track incorrectly set, though, a fault which made the Countach feel unstable under heavy braking and prone to oversteer when cornered near the limit. On the road, we had no trouble controlling the errant tail when it did step out of line, but within the safe confines of MIRA's test track, where very high cornering speeds are possible, it would have been all too easy to spin the car.

Under more normal conditions the Countach behaves extremely well. The light but high geared steering has good feel and allows the car to be placed with great accuracy. The car handles bumpy surfaces well: there is little kick-back from the steering and no grounding – faults which often spoil ultra fast sports cars on country roads. Minimal roll, excellent adhesion and good response to the helm allow the car to be steered through a series of bends quickly and safely.

Heavy braking from high speed provoked slight judder and graunching noises from the discs, but there was no sign of fade. Although they feel dead and fairly heavy, they coped

well with the formidable task of repeatedly pulling the Countach down from speeds of 130 mph to 40 mph or less.

There is a surprising amount of luggage space. The main compartment is behind the engine in the tail – a deep square box that will hold more than enough suitcases for a long weekend. There are also small spaces above and around the spare wheel in the front, and the gaps behind the seats if they are not pushed right back.

Headroom is restricted for anyone over 6 ft tall but, mainly because the steering column is adjustable for length as well as height, the driving position is the best we have yet encountered in a Lamborghini. There is plenty of leg and elbow room and the seats are comfortable and hold you tightly in place on corners.

The pedals take some getting used to as they are offset to the left and the brake pedal goes below the accelerator under heavy braking, making heel and toe changes tricky. But Lamborghini can adjust the pedal positions to suit customers.

Two stalks – one each side of the steering column – incorporate most of the minor switchgear (wash/wipe, headlamp flash/dip indicators) and are within fingertip reach. The seat belts, however, are awful – very difficult to adjust and untidy when not in use.

Seeing out is a good deal easier than the space-age styling suggests from outside. You sit well forward and the nose dips sharply out of sight, which can be a problem when parking. The rear three-quarter view is completely obscured, but you soon learn to adapt to this by approaching road junctions at right angles, as in a van, and looking through the side window. The mirror view aft is quite adequate.

Internal reflections on the windscreen – so often a problem with steeply raked screens – are not too apparent, but any form of road film is; it pays to keep the windscreen washer well topped up and to use it often.

The interior is tastefully furnished in typical Italian style – matt black velvet-covered facia and polished aluminium surround for the instruments – and is well finished. Stray reflections in daylight spoil what is otherwise an attractive and effective instrument layout (sloping glasses are needed here).

With only the oil radiator mounted forward of the passenger compartment the air conditioning is not worked so hard as on many more conventional cars as hot air is not flowing rearwards from the water radiators. In all but the hottest weather it was not needed, but when called upon to do so it releases a strong blast of cold air.

The Countach is certainly a very impressive machine. Even allowing for the below-par engine, the Countach compares well with its rivals and sets standards that on the whole are commensurate with its price tag. For a show car turned road car, and considering its futuristic styling, it is a good deal more practical than we expected.

How do you get out if it rolls? You push the windscreen out!

At the time of going to press the future of Lamborghini was uncertain, the company being held in a mild form of receivership following their failure to meet the commitment with BMW to build the bodies for the German company's mid-engined M1.

The only notable change to the Countach after our 1975 test has been the S version with even wider wheels and tyres.

GENERAL SPECIFICATION

Engine

Cylinders	12 in vee
Capacity	3 929 cc
Bore/stroke	82 × 62 mm
Cooling	water
Block	Elektron light alloy
Head	Elektron light alloy
Valves	dohc per bank
Compression	10·5:1
Carburettor	6 Weber 45DCOE twin-choke
Bearings	7 main
Max power	375 bhp (DIN) at 8 000 rpm
Max torque	268 lb-ft (DIN) at 5 000 rpm

Transmission

Type	5-speed manual
Internal ratios and mph/1000 rpm	
Top	0·755:1/23·7
4th	0·990:1/18·6
3rd	1·310:1/14·1
2nd	1·769:1/10·4
1st	2·256:1/8·1
Rev	2·134:1
Final drive	4·080:1

Body/Chassis

Construction	tubular steel chassis and aluminium coachwork

Suspension

Front	independent by wishbones, coil springs, telescopic dampers, anti-roll bar; fully adjustable
Rear	independent by wishbones, coil springs, telescopic dampers, anti-roll bar; fully adjustable

Steering

Type	rack and pinion
Assistance	no

Brakes

Front	ventilated discs
Rear	ventilated discs
Servo	yes
Circuit	split

Wheels/Tyres

Type	cast magnesium, 7½J × 14 in (front); 9J × 14 in (rear)
Tyres	Michelin XWX 205/70 VR14 (front); 215/70 VR14 (rear)

Electrical

Battery	12v, 66 a-h
Earth	negative
Generator	70 amp alternator
Fuses	16
Headlights	4 × 55W

PERFORMANCE DATA

Maximum speeds

	mph
Top (estimated)	175
4th	149
3rd	115
2nd	83
1st	65

Acceleration from rest

mph	sec
0-30	2·7
0-40	3·4
0-50	4·4
0-60	5·6
0-70	7·5
0-80	9·0
0-90	11·1
0-100	13·1
0-110	15·9
0-120	20·3
Standing ¼ mile	14·1
Standing km	25·2

Acceleration in top

mph	sec
30-50	—
40-60	—
50-70	12·0
60-80	12·6
70-90	10·3
80-100	11·0
90-110	11·4
100-120	13·7

Fuel consumption

Touring* (estimated)	11 mpg
Overall	10 mpg
Tank capacity	26·4 gal
Max range	290 miles

*Consumption midway between 30 mph and maximum speed less 5% allowance for acceleration.
Maximum range is based on touring consumption.

JAGUAR XJ-S

Despite what it is – an outrageously large and heavy two-plus-two – the Jaguar XJ-S is a magnificent car, not just for what it does, but for the way it does it. The XJ-S combines a startling performance with exceptional smoothness and tractability and a standard of refinement that few cars can match. Others may be quicker; some handle better; a Rolls-Royce has more prestige; many have more room; quite a few are prettier. But none (other Jaguars apart) are smoother, quieter or more flexible.

In concept, the latest Jaguar must be regarded as a splendid anachronism. For a start, it was conceived when there were fewer speed limits, and fuel was relatively cheap and apparently abundant.

Much the same result could be achieved with less weight, capacity or complication, and thus better fuel consumption – the Lotus Elite shows the way. Yet we do not doubt that throughout the world there are many people who have both the taste and finance to appreciate the skill and technology that has gone into this superb machine, even if it does belong to a bygone era.

The heart of the XJ-S is, of course, Jaguar's superb 5·3 litre V12. In fuel injected form it produces 285 bhp (DIN) at 5500 rpm while the torque curve peaks at 294 lb-ft (DIN) at 3500 rpm.

The engine is of all-alloy construction, with single overhead camshafts per bank, Lucas Opus electronic ignition, Lucas fuel injection – and splendid ribbed covers over the camshafts.

The manual four-speed transmission of the test car is Jaguar's own, and the suspension follows XJ practice. The twin wishbones at the front are angled to give anti-dive characteristics, springing is by coils with concentric shock absorbers. The geometry and roll-bar stiffness have been altered to suit the new car and the special Dunlop SP Sport Super 205/70VR15 tyres.

At the back the familiar Jaguar independent system is employed, with lower tubular transverse wishbones, fixed length drive-shafts acting as upper links and two radius arms running forward to mounting points on the body. Twin coil spring/damper units each side are located fore and aft of the driveshaft, and for the first time an anti-roll bar is fitted. The powerful braking system is by 11 in ventilated discs at the front and smaller discs inboard at the rear. The rack and pinion steering has Adwest power assistance.

As we were unable to carry out a maximum speed run, we have quoted the manufacturer's claimed top speed (155 mph). The ease with which the car reached an indicated 149 mph on one occasion would suggest that the maximum is certainly well above 150 mph.

The standing start acceleration is equally impressive; such figures as 6·7 sec to 60 mph and 16·2 sec to 100 mph are electrifying times; only the Aston Martin V8, various Porsches and a handful of exotics are any quicker.

But pure performance, impressive though the figures may be, is just one aspect of the XJ-S. What makes it so special is the way the performance is achieved. From the moment the pre-engaged starter whirrs the engine into life, aided by automatic enrichment from the fuel injection system, followed by an undramatic warm-up period, the V12 pro-

vides instant and uncannily smooth power – in any gear, at any speed and revs, on up to the maximum in top.

There is no temperament, no fuss or bother, no abrupt change, no 'coming on the cam,' in fact none of the characteristics which are often the hallmarks of cars with equal or better performance but with more highly tuned and stressed engines. The engine is so flexible that it is possible to pull away cleanly and vigorously from a walking pace in top.

This potency and flexibility is allied to a smoothness and quietness that, to use the words of one of our testers, is 'miraculous'. We would expect a V12 to be smooth, but that of the XJ-S is exceptional, while it is so well muffled that passengers are often unaware of the high speed at which they are travelling. As revs rise there is just a slight change in engine note, but it only becomes really noticeable above 5 500 rpm – and we cannot see many drivers using such revs very often. With such massive torque low down you do not need to extend the engine, 70 mph in top is a very restful 2 800 rpm, at which point the engine just emits a muted hum.

As expected the XJ-S is very thirsty, as our overall consumption of 12·8 mpg confirms, although it is no worse than that of other cars of similar performance and weight. Note, however, that the lighter Porsche 911 lux Targa, with a smaller, more efficient engine returned 19·8 mpg overall, and the (slower) Lotus 21·7 mpg.

One of the less endearing aspects of the XJ-S is the transmission. The clutch is a little heavy and unprogressive, and the change is stiff and notchy if you rush it so it pays to ease

the lever around rather than snatch at it.

One of our constant criticisms of Jaguars is that their power steering has, up to now, been too light. That fitted to the XJ-S has more resistance but no more feel than that of other models – but the extra weight is a move in the right direction. Otherwise we have no complaints, for it is direct and responsive with no slop or lost motion, and parking is easy.

With fat, 70 series tyres and a sophisticated and developed suspension the roadholding is all you would expect – the grip in the wet from the Dunlop tyres is remarkable, although it is possible to break traction and spin the wheels, even after a leisurely getaway. The supple suspension absorbs irregularities extremely well so that the XJ-S is not put off line by bumps in mid-corner.

The handling is exemplary and the car always feels well balanced and safe. You have to be cornering very hard before the normal mild understeer changes to predictable and controllable oversteer under power. Lifting off or braking in a corner simply tightens the line without any drama. When the tail does break away – and that requires a fair amount of throttle – the XJ-S can be untidy in that, possibly due to the limited slip differential, poor steering feel or a slightly too stiff anti-roll bar, the rear end tends to lurch around.

The XJ-S is fun to drive fast along country roads, for its taut, balanced handling, excellent traction, lack of roll and precise (if feelless) steering allow you to hustle the car along without drama. It is possible that the Mercedes and some of the more expensive exotic cars can and do behave even better, but this is only noticeable at limits which few owners are ever going to reach.

The power steering naturally takes all the effort out of parking, and the turning circle is a commendable 34 ft or so, comparatively small for what is a long and bulky car. The front spoiler and general shape not only prevent the nose lifting at speed but also seem to keep the XJ-S tracking straight in high cross-winds.

The XJ-S has the brakes to cope with its weight and performance. There are 11·2 in ventilated discs at the front, 10·38 in inboard discs at the rear, twin hydraulic circuits, one for each end, a pressure differential warning actuator which shuts off a faulty circuit in case of failure, and naturally a servo.

In use the brakes live up to their specification. They are powerful and progressive, but possibly the most impressive aspect of their performance was that, in conjunction with the excellent grip from the tyres, they pulled this heavy car to a standstill with a deceleration of over 1 g – in the wet. Some cars cannot achieve that in the dry. Nor did they show any signs of fade during our test, which involved 20 stops, one minute apart, from a speed of 100 mph.

Minor instruments on the XJ-S follow aircraft practice

In contrast the handbrake could only manage a disappointing 0·22 g – below the legal limit.

There is plenty of space for those in the front seats, but the rear is cramped. Not only is leg and footroom severely restricted, but headroom is limited even for short people and width is just about adequate due to intrusive armrests – but shoulder width is reasonable.

The boot is deep and square and looks quite big; it swallowed 10·9 cu ft of our test luggage. But it is shaped so that there is quite a lot of room for squashy bags but not all that much for ordinary suitcases.

At most speeds the suspension permits some slight trembling which can turn into small-bump harshness at low speeds, but these are characteristics that indicate firm damping and a taut suspension. There is also some float at speed over undulations – waves on a motorway for example. Otherwise the ride is up to the usual very high Jaguar standards.

The XJ-S will cope with quite rough surfaces and severe irregularities with aplomb and no trace of sogginess. Add to this the lack of bump-thump and tyre noises and the ride becomes remarkable. The lack of roll, dive, squat, pitch or bounce increase even more a passenger's peace of mind.

The XJ-S is designed to provide maximum comfort for two in the front, and in this on the whole it succeeds. The seats are comfortable and provide the right sort of support in the right places, while the extensive range of fore-and-aft adjustment, the reclining backrest and the reach adjustable steering column meant that most drivers could find a good position (although one or two would have liked some form of seat height/tilt control).

The major controls are well sited, the pedals allowing 'heeling-and-toeing' and the gearlever being within easy reach.

Some of our testers thought that Jaguar had spoilt the styling of the instruments by surrounding them with a thin, painted silver line which made them look cheap. They are otherwise attractive to look at, well lit via a rheostat, and reasonably comprehensive.

Flanking the four smaller instruments in the middle are the large speedometer plus odometer and trip meter on the left (reading to 160 mph) and the matching tachometer, red-lined at 6500 rpm, on the right.

The four smaller instruments are clever and unusual in that they are arranged so that the needles move vertically, and with everything working correctly (and the tank half full) they form a single yellow line across the panel, so that only the briefest glance is needed to check that all is well, in accordance with aircraft practice. Reading from left to right the individual instruments are the water temperature gauge, the oil pressure gauge, the fuel gauge and the voltmeter. Above them is a battery of no fewer than 18 warning lights.

The XJ-S comes as standard with a fully automatic air conditioning unit made by Delanair. This is controlled by two rotary switches, one to select temperature (from 65° to 85°F), the other to control the function from 'off', through 'lo', 'auto', 'hi' to 'def' (frost).

In practice the system does not seem to

give all that it promises. In the cold weather during the test period there was no chance properly to assess the cooling mode (although a quick test gave a really cold blast from the centre vent) but on the 'auto' setting (or the 'hi' or 'lo' setting for that matter) the flow from the vents at each end of the facia is poor so that it is difficult to get warm feet and a cool face, which leads to stuffiness, in spite of a temperature differential between upper and lower circuits.

Jaguar are masters at suppressing noise, vibration and harshness and the XJ-S is a brilliant example of their technological achievement. Even so, individual noises can be identified from the general light murmer: there is the gearbox whine in first and second, road noise is sometimes noticeable at speed on some surfaces, the power steering hisses when parking or manoeuvrring, and the engine note rises at high revs, of course. But many other manufacturers would be glad to get their noise levels down even to these standards, and they must envy the lack of wind noise (no louder, it seems, at 120 mph than it is at 70 mph), the well-muffled bump-thump and the suppression of tyre roar at low speeds in town.

We expected the rear three-quarter pillars and curved Dino-style fins to create blind spots, but they are far enough back not to be a problem. Yet the windscreen pillars get in the way, and the windscreen header rail is low and far back, giving a beetle-browed impression and a slight feeling of claustrophobia. And the side windows get very dirty in foul weather.

The two-speed wipers clear an effectively large area of the windscreen. We like the flick-wipe facility, but feel that an intermittent wipe, especially one with variable delay, would be far more useful. Cheaper cars have it – why not the XJ-S?

As befits the price and image, the XJ-S is well equipped, with such still comparatively rare items as air conditioning, leather upholstery, electric window operation, central locking, a radio, alloy wheels, and adjustable steering. Omissions include a fuel filler lock (optional) and the aforementioned wiper delay.

Gone from the facia is the traditional wooden instrument panel. The new facia, trimmed in black and matt silver, is attractive and functional, while the rest of the interior is subtly and discreetly trimmed and finished: stylish without being ostentatious. The seats look particularly sumptuous, and there is a lovely smell of real leather.

The finish in general is to a high standard: all carpets and other items fit well, the seams on the seats and elsewhere are straight, the doors shut with a satisfying clonk and the shut lines are even.

The only real criticism that could be levelled at the XJ-S is that it's dated in concept. Like Concorde, it is a superb technological achievement, with perhaps a questionable future.

Having said that, we must emphasise just what a magnificent car the XJ-S is. Some rivals may be better than the Jaguar in one or two ways, but none have the unique combination of qualities that makes the XJ-S, for us, the best of all. And although it is an expensive car, it is still remarkable value for money.

The XJ-S was launched in September 1975, initially only with automatic transmission, and it was not until February 1976 that a manual transmission version was available for *Motor* to road test. At the time of writing it remains in production in virtually unchanged form.

GENERAL SPECIFICATION

Engine

Cylinders	12 in vee
Capacity	5 343 cc
Bore/stroke	90 × 70 mm
Cooling	water
Block	aluminium alloy
Head	aluminium alloy
Valves	sohc per bank
Compression	9:1
Fuel injection	Lucas
Bearings	7 main
Max power	285 bhp (DIN) at 5 500 rpm
Max torque	294 lb-ft (DIN) at 3 500 rpm

Transmission

Type	4-speed manual

Internal ratios and mph/1000 rpm

Top	1·000:1/24·7
3rd	1·389:1/17·8
2nd	1·905:1/13·0
1st	3·238:1/7·6
Rev	3·428:1
Final drive	3·07:1

Body/Chassis

Construction	unitary, all steel

Suspension

Front	independent by double wishbones, coil springs, anti-roll bar
Rear	independent by lower wishbones, driveshafts as upper links, radius arms, twin coil spring/ damper units per side

Steering

Type	rack and pinion
Assistance	yes

Brakes

Front	11·2 in ventilated discs
Rear	10·4 in discs
Servo	yes
Circuit	split, front/rear

Wheels/Tyres

Type	alloy, 6JK × 15 in
Tyres	Dunlop SP Super 205/70 VR15

Electrical

Battery	12v, 68 a-h
Earth	negative
Generator	alternator
Fuses	12
Headlights	2 × Cibie quartz halogen

PERFORMANCE DATA

Maximum speeds

	mph	rpm
Top	155	6 275
3rd	116	6 500
2nd	84	6 500
1st	50	6 500

Acceleration from rest

mph	sec
0-30	2·8
0-40	3·8
0-50	5·1
0-60	6·7
0-70	8·4
0-80	10·5
0-90	13·4
0-100	16·2
0-110	20·2
0-120	25·8
Standing ¼ mile	15·0
Standing km	27·2

Acceleration in top

mph	sec
10-30	7·5
20-40	6·8
30-50	6·6
40-60	6·8
50-70	6·9
60-80	7·1
70-90	7·2
80-100	8·0
90-110	8·6
100-120	10·3

Fuel consumption

Touring (estimated)*	14·4 mpg
Overall	12·8 mpg
Tank capacity	20·0 gal
Max range	288 miles

*Consumption midway between 30 mph and maximum speed, less 5% allowance for acceleration. Maximum range is based on touring consumption.

MASERATI Merak

Wealthy buyers of expensive sports cars, wanting to take clients to lunch or friends to dinner, sometimes complain if their vehicle lacks occasional rear seats. Mid-engined cars are often heavily condemned for this deficiency – rather unfairly, in our view, since the whole philosophy of the sports car makes some loss in efficient space utilisation a worthwhile sacrifice for the best possible roadholding and traction. Nevertheless such criticisms have goaded the smaller, mostly Italian, makers of expensive machinery into evolving various experimental and production mid-engined 2 + 2s, and one result is the Maserati Merak tested here. Introduced at the 1972 Paris show, it is a derivative of the existing Bora, having exactly the same wheelbase, platform, bonnet, doors, double-wishbone independent suspension at each end and fully powered Citroen-style brakes.

But, whereas the Bora is powered by a 4·7-litre V8, the Merak is equipped with a 3-litre V6 – an enlarged version of the unit fitted to the Citroen SM – and the saving in engine length has been used to extend the cockpit rearwards and place in it a pair of small occasional rear seats. And whereas the Bora has a glassed-in fastback tail, the Merak's engine is covered by a flat rear deck ending in a small lip, but 'flying buttresses' curving downwards and rearwards from the cockpit roof complete the inverted-saucer profile. Aesthetically the result is an exceptionally striking, crowd-pulling car, considerably more handsome, in the opinion of all our staff, than the Bora from which it is derived.

At first the Merak was consistently difficult to start from cold despite being returned to the concessionaires for remedial attention several times, but the trouble was eventually traced to a faulty radio switch draining current from the battery overnight. With the fault fixed, the engine always started promptly from cold after a couple of pumps on the accelerator pedal to prime the Weber carburettors.

The engine is simply an enlarged version of the four-cam V6 used for the Citroen SM: by retaining the 75 mm stroke but enlarging the bore from 87 mm to 91·6 mm its capacity has been increased from the 2670 cc of the SM version to 2965 cc for the Merak. Using three double-choke Weber carburettors and a slightly lowered compression ratio its output has been raised from the 178 (DIN) bhp of the Citroen unit with Bosch fuel injection to 190 bhp at 6000 rpm and maximum torque is up from 164 lb-ft at 4000 rpm to 188 lb-ft at the same engine speed.

This engine pulled without hesitation during the warm-up period, idled regularly when hot and started promptly for the rest of the day. At certain low speeds, particularly around 3000 rpm the exhaust note takes on an uneven waffly note – perhaps due to the uneven firing intervals – which makes the engine sound a little rough. But at all other times it was exceptionally smooth right up to its 6500 rpm limit, and without being noisy in an anti-social way emitted a magnificent blare at high revs liked by everyone who drove the car. But at high cruising speeds in the 100-110 mph range the sound of the engine settled back to a subdued burble.

Below 1500 rpm – equivalent to nearly 33 mph in fifth and nearly 25 mph in fourth – the engine will not pull without hesitation, but above that speed it urges the car smoothly

forward. Although real power does not begin to come in until above 3000 rpm, there is no particular point at which the unit really gets into its stride. There is a slight hesitation – again at around 3000 rpm – if the throttle is opened slightly but sharply: it does not occur if the accelerator pedal is firmly floored.

With a 0-60 mph acceleration time of 7·5 sec and a 0-100 mph time of 19·9 sec the Merak does not have absolute top of the league performance but is still pretty quick. And as the engine sounds so relaxed it gets along with deceptive rapidity, cruising with a total lack of fuss at 110 mph or more. The acceleration time from 30-50 mph of 9·5 sec in fifth is not particularly impressive, but fifth is essentially an overdrive cruising gear, and in fourth the same speed interval is covered in only 6·5 sec.

According to Maserati's rather over-heated slide-rules, the Merak should be capable of nearly 150 mph, although at the 6500 rpm red line the maximum theoretical speed is just over 140 mph. In these troubled times there is now nowhere we can go to make a proper confirmation of such claims, but we were able to pull 6200 rpm on one occasion, indicated on a rev-counter slightly slow at this speed, with the car still accelerating, so we do believe the car is capable of a genuine 140 mph.

At steady speeds the Merak is surprisingly frugal in its use of fuel, an objective finding – the consumption at 100 mph is as good as 20·2 mpg – which is subjectively confirmed by the small throttle openings necessary to maintain high speeds in fifth. This leads to our touring value of 22·1 mpg and a rather theoretical maximum range from the 18·6-gallon tank of over 400 miles. But the car's considerable weight, the tendency to make full use of its acceleration, the inevitable proportion of town driving and possible excessive acceleration enrichment from the Weber carburettors all combined to reduce this figure to a distinctly poor 13·2 mpg. On some journeys the consumption fell almost to 10 mpg and it never rose above 15 mpg.

Unlike the Bora with a transaxle and five-speed gearbox made by ZF, the Merak has the unit built for the Citroen SM which is far lighter and less ponderous to use. In the Merak, however, it is not quite as outstanding as it is in the SM, mainly because of the excessively heavy spring loading that has to be overcome to get the lever into first or second. And as is all too common with cars of this sort, the clutch is ridiculously heavy, requiring a 60 lb load to depress it. But at the same time the change is precise, light and unobstructive, and most of our drivers soon adapted to its faults and found it a delight to use on the road. It did resist the very fastest of changes required for our standing-start acceleration tests with a little crunch, es-

pecially into third, but with a crunch as much in the linkage as the gears.

Maximum speeds of 35 mph, 53 mph, 77 mph and 109 mph are attainable in the four lower gears which thus have a sensible spread of ratios. Third is ideal for over-taking, fourth for fast driving on roads with some bends and fifth for relaxed cruising.

For ordinary driving on public roads the Merak corners like all good mid-engined sports cars in having a responsiveness and go-where-you-point-it precision which is vastly superior to anything achieved by the best front-engined models. Nor is it, as was the Bora, in the least put off line by bumpy surfaces. It is stable, too, at very high speeds on the straight.

Try a little harder and you discover that it – again like most other mid-engined cars – tends to understeer when powered through a corner but to tuck into oversteer if the accelerator is released in the middle of it, but the Merak differs slightly from others of its kind since it will also oversteer, gently and controllably, in tightish bends up to about 60 mph if the throttles are kept open. The huge Michelin radial tyres, 185 section at the front, 205 at the rear – on 7 in trims give reserves of cornering power seldom likely to be exceeded outside the confines of a private test track.

All this applies to dry conditions. We had little opportunity to drive the car in the wet, but from occasional encounters with slippery patches we feel that the tail might be a little skittish under acceleration in rainy weather. From experience with other mid-engined cars we would also expect the accentuation of the understeer characteristic and a slight tendency for the front tyres to aquaplane on puddles.

The car is less endearing at parking speeds. Although the rack and pinion steering (which has no power assistance) is light on the move with good feel – and perhaps a little kickback – it is also rather indirect, and at low speeds, heavy. In addition the lock is very poor.

Maserati have, in our view, moved in just

the wrong way towards the partial adoption of the famous hydraulic and hydropneumatic systems pioneered by their parent company, Citroen. It is the Citroen hydropneumatic springs that the Merak needs to cure its harsh and uncomfortable ride, but instead the hydraulic pump, accumulator and elaborate plumbing has been fitted merely to operate the pop-up headlamps and a braking system with all the Citroen faults and a few others besides.

We cannot repeat too often our basic criticism of this system, which on the Merak, as on most other Citroens, requires far too little pedal pressure – a 50 lb load gave a stop of over 0·8 g – and far too little pedal movement. The resultant over-sensitivity makes it very difficult for enthusiasts to heel and toe without jerks – though it can be done after a little practice – but more important makes it almost impossible for any driver to bring the car smoothly to rest when braking hard on a bumpy surface. Each time the car hits a bump the driver's leg is jerked forward on to the pedal, locking or nearly locking the wheels so that the car comes to a halt in a series of untidy screeches.

To be fair, we found it possible to adapt partially to the system, which with a suitable delicate use of the right foot proved capable of clawing the car down from a high speed in an impressive way so long as the road surface was reasonably smooth and the braking not too hard. And with four big discs – the rear ones mounted inboard – there was no fade during our driving or tests, nor was the system much affected by the watersplash.

But the best deceleration that the system could achieve was a very indifferent 0·89 g, the brakes always pulled to one side during a hard stop and occasionally a rear wheel locked up under a light pedal pressure, putting the car frighteningly off line. The handbrake, too, would not hold the car on the 1-in-4 slope and managed a pathetic – and illegal – 0·14 g maximum deceleration.

Both front seats have a generous range of

fore-and-aft adjustment giving ample leg-room for the tallest of occupants. Even when these seats are in their foremost positions, however, the legroom behind them is very limited as is the headroom so there is barely space for adults. An average-sized child of 10 travelling in the rear of the car will probably prefer to sit crosswise, draping his legs over the central tunnel. Moreover it is difficult to get into the rear at all as the front seat backrests do not tilt far enough forward.

On the passenger's side there is a very small lockable glove compartment with a shallow shelf in front of it. No other space for maps and oddments is provided except for a pair of small pockets formed in the armrests. The boot however is surprisingly capacious, and accepted 6·6 cu ft of our suitcases.

Despite the fully independent suspension all round and the low centre of gravity – which would allow soft springs to be used without creating much roll – the Merak's ride is harsh and excessively firm. This is particularly noticeable on highways with transverse-ridged surfaces which can set up a jerky and unpleasant shaking motion. Although the movement of the car is well damped and controlled on undulations, it is very uncomfortable on really bumpy surfaces, shaking the driver about too much to make fast driving easy.

The front seats are comfortable with adequate lumbar support in their reclining backrests, but we did not like the slippery leather upholstery which accentuated the lack of lateral support – much needed in a car with such a high cornering power.

Most unusual for a foreign car, the Merak's steering column is adjustable for both reach and rake, a facility which certainly does help to make the driving position comfortable for different shapes and sizes of people. But the wheel does not tilt upwards enough for tall drivers and the locking lever did not always hold it securely in position. All the pedals and the remote-control gearlever are well laid out, however, and a useful rest for the left foot is built into the toeboard.

The principal features of the instrument panel are the dials of the speedometer and matching rev-counter mounted directly in front of the driver on either side of a small oil-pressure gauge. These two main instruments are attractive in appearance and of reasonable size but their glasses create unwanted reflections and they are mounted too low to be seen easily by tall drivers. Above the central console, is a clock and a battery of auxiliary instruments monitoring fuel tank contents, oil temperature, water temperature and battery voltage.

Like many expensive cars the Merak has a high scuttle and waist and bulges at the sides and so is not the easiest of cars to manoeuvre in a confined space especially if the driver is short. But forward visibility is good, the wiper pattern is fair – although the blades need to be rather longer – and there is an excellent view directly to the rear where the tip of the car is delineated by the small lip or spoiler at the end of the tail. The three-quarter rear visibility, often the Achilles' heel of mid-engined cars, is fair, and the lights gave a good blaze of light both when dipped and when on main beam.

The rather crude heating system is partly controlled by a switch which selects between outside or recirculated air. There is a temperature control lever, but it is so insensitive in action that it is effectively either on or off. All distribution has to be done by opening or closing the plastic flaps covering the circular vents under the windscreen, in the footwells and on the central console. As there is no fresh-air ventilation it is impossible to obtain a comfortable condition with cool air to the face and warm air to the feet and there is very little throughput without the booster fan. But the heater was powerful, and its booster fan was able to clear the screen of mist very quickly. An electric rear window demister is also fitted.

Our test car was fitted with the optional air conditioning system. This proved itself capable of blowing a welcome breeze of cool air through the central console vent, but of course would not work when the heating system was operating.

In most respects this Maserati is a quiet car. At a standstill the sharp clatter of the hydraulic pump can be heard every now and then as it cuts in, and the engine rattles slightly when idling. But even when extended in the gears, the splendid noise it makes is not excessively loud, and at high cruising speeds it is quiet. The almost complete absence of wind noise when travelling fast contributes greatly to the relaxed and unfussed character of the car, but some bump-thump and roar on coarse surfaces is generated by the tyres.

The exterior paintwork is good and at first sight the interior finish seems to the same

standard but there is some uneven trim in places and the central console vent seems carelessly located, as it touches the fresh-air/recirculating switch. There would appear to be even less attention to detail in those places not immediately visible to the naked eye judging by the 2 in of water which filled the footwell on the driver's side when we passed through the MIRA watersplash.

After this 1974 road test the Merak became, in 1975, the Merak SS, with power increased to 220 bhp, longer-legged gearing, and suspension revisions. In a 1977 test, we found the acceleration at low speeds a little poorer than the 1974 car's, a consequence no doubt of the taller gearing, but it was faster at the top end. The handling was even better than before, and the ride comfort somewhat improved.

GENERAL SPECIFICATION

Engine
Cylinders	6 in vee
Capacity	2965 cc
Bore/stroke	91·6 × 75 mm
Cooling	water
Block	alloy
Head	alloy
Valves	dohc per bank
Compression	8·75:1
Carburettor	3 Weber 42DCNF twin-choke
Bearings	4 main
Max power	190 bhp (DIN) at 6000 rpm
Max torque	188 lb-ft (DIN) at 4000 rpm

Transmission
Type	5-speed manual
Internal ratios and mph/1000 rpm	
Top	0·73:1/21·6
4th	0·94:1/16·8
3rd	1·32:1/11·9
2nd	1·94:1/8·2
1st	2·92:1/5·4
Rev	3·15:1
Final drive	4·85:1

Body/Chassis
Construction	integral, steel

Suspension
Front	independent by wishbones, coil springs, anti-roll bar
Rear	independent by wishbones, coil springs, anti-roll bar

Steering
Type	rack and pinion
Assistance	no

Brakes
Front	11 in ventilated discs
Rear	11·8 in ventilated discs
Servo	hydraulic, pressurised
Circuit	dual

Wheels/Tyres
Type	alloy, 7 × 15 in
Tyres	185/70 VR15 (front); 205/70 VR15 (rear)

Electrical
Battery	12v, 72 a-h
Earth	negative
Generator	alternator
Fuses	12
Headlights	2 quartz halogen

PERFORMANCE DATA

Maximum speeds
	mph	rpm
Top (see text) ...	140	6480
4th	109	6500
3rd	77	6500
2nd	53	6500
1st	35	6500

Acceleration from rest
mph	sec
0-30	2·6
0-40	4·3
0-50	5·5
0-60	7·5
0-70	9·7
0-80	12·3
0-90	15·6
0-100...	19·9
0-110...	25·2
0-120...	—
Standing ¼ mile	15·7
Standing km..	28·8

Acceleration in
mph	top sec	4th
10-30	—	—
20-40	—	—
30-50	9·4	6·5
40-60	9·5	6·5
50-70	9·4	6·5
60-80	9·6	6·5
70-90	10·3	6·9
80-100	11·6	7·8
90-110	13·1	9·4
100-120	—	—

Fuel consumption
Touring	22·1 mpg
Overall	13·2 mpg
Tank capacity	18·6 gal
Max range	411 miles

*Consumption midway between 30 mph and maximum speed less 5% allowance for acceleration.
Maximum range is based on touring consumption.

FERRARI 308GTB

It was Ferrari themselves who axed the Dino 246, that much-loved mid-engined two-seater classic with impeccably precise and responsive handling. They probably regretted the decision, for few have greeted its successor – the 308 GT4 2 plus 2 – with the same fervour. The 308's larger engine with eight instead of six cylinders certainly gives more torque and an impressive performance but the gearbox is indifferent, the steering rather dead and low-geared, the handling less responsive than the 246's, and the rear seats too occasional to be regarded seriously. Perhaps heeding these criticisms Ferrari introduced an additional model, the 308 GTB, a short wheelbase two-seater version of the basic car which with its grooved flanks bears more than a passing resemblance to the old 246, although with far crisper and more modern lines. The shape was created by Pininfarina in a wind tunnel and is said to give a lower drag coefficient and improved stability at high speed (the car will do over 150 mph). What is more the body is made of glassfibre, making the 308 GTB the first road-going Ferrari to use this material. Its chassis, though, is a steel, mostly tubular structure, and its suspension the same all-independent double-wishbone system used

for the 2 + 2, with the same braking system incorporating four ventilated discs.

Everything we heard about this exciting new model suggested that it was the 246 reborn with even better handling and radically superior refinement and comfort. Could any car be that good?

Undoubtedly the most powerful initial impression received, when we first drove an example to find out, was that made by the engine. As for the 2 + 2 car, this 2 927 cc light alloy V8 power unit is mounted transversely behind the driver just ahead of the rear wheels which it drives through a Mini-style train of transfer gears to a transmission assembly located behind it. With two belt-driven overhead camshafts for each bank of cylinders, four twin-choke Weber carburettors and a compression ratio of 8·8:1, it develops 255 (DIN) bhp at 7 700 rpm and 209·8 lb-ft of torque at 5 000 rpm – just the same as for the bigger model, although the engine has dry rather than wet sump lubrication.

The result is, quite simply, magnificent. It hurls the car forward with an utterly smooth, wholly effortless howl, in the true Ferrari manner. It reaches its 7 700 rpm limit with so little fuss or sense of strain as to make the tachometer an important item of equipment since no rev-limiter is fitted.

The engine also behaves perfectly in town, as it has ample torque at low revs. In fact it pulls without hesitation from about 1 200 rpm in fifth – a remarkable achievement for such a highly tuned unit – although it does run into a gurgle-and-hesitation region around 1 800 rpm before starting to pull firmly ahead again at just over 2 000 rpm. Nor does the power come in abruptly, but starts a long steady surge from 2 500 rpm onwards and shows no signs of tailing off at high revs.

Subjectively the car feels immensely quick and its performance is certain to delight every owner. By our objective measurements, however, the car was a little slower than the 2 + 2 308 we tested, though it should be a little quicker as Ferrari claim it is

lighter. Even so, 0-60 mph and 0-100 mph acceleration times of 6·8 sec and 16·5 sec respectively mean that another Ferrari – or maybe a Porsche – will be among the few cars on the road likely to keep up with the GTB.

Nor is it left spluttering after being baulked by a slower car, with a fifth gear 50-70 mph acceleration time of only 7·2 sec – better than many cars can do in third, always assuming that they can reach 70 mph in this gear. We were unable to check the maximum speed, but something comfortably over 150 mph (Ferrari claim 158 mph) seems entirely credible.

Magnificent though it is, the 308's engine is not perfect. Despite its single-pipe exhaust and improved intake silencing, it is still a little noisy – noticeably more so for the driver than the passenger. Few are likely to object to the splendid sounds it makes when gunned through the gears, but it has a boom period at around 6000 rpm and it is not as quiet as it should be when cruising at high speeds in fifth.

Moreover, for reasons we can not fathom it loses the edge of its smoothness when the air conditioning unit is in operation as well as a little performance (although that we *can* understand). Perhaps the engagement of the air conditioning unit creates a sound-conducting path, for its use also makes the engine slightly more noisy, increasing the prominence of the whine made by the various valve trains and transfer gears. Despite these criticisms, we definitely feel that the 308 GTB wins Round One of its contest with the 246, although only marginally for the older car has a very fine engine too.

Round Two is even closer, for the GTB's gearchange is very similar to the 246's – it is significantly better than the gearchange of the 2 + 2 model we tested. The change of this five-speed gearbox is rather stiff and notchy when the gearbox oil is cold, and remains a little notchy for leisurely in-town changes even when it is hot.

The dog-leg movement involved in getting from first (which is away from the driver and back) to second also takes some getting used to. But the feeling of accomplishment which comes when the change is mastered is very rewarding, and the gearbox is a joy to use on the open road: the prescence of the gate is soon forgotten and the faster you change the easier and lighter the movement becomes.

None of this is made any easier, however, by the action of the clutch which has a very long travel and has to be pressed right to the floor if grating noises – especially when selecting second – are to be avoided. The clutch has the further nasty habit – very embarrassing, conceivably expensive, in a car of this sort – of momentarily sticking during fast changes at high rpm in its fully

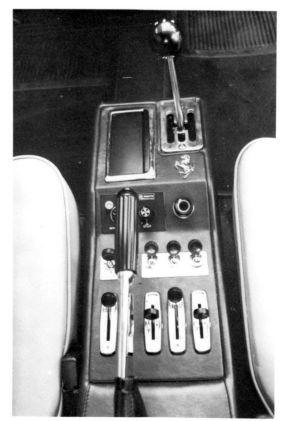

The gearchange pattern is clearly defined by the metal gate

better. To begin with it had the go-were-you-point-it precision that we liked so much in the 246. Up to quite high cornering speeds you do not have to worry about oversteer and understeer, you just steer and the car follows without fuss or drama. The steering itself, a trifle low-geared but reasonably light at parking speeds, is precise and has good feel once on the move.

Try a little harder and the car responds with some mild understeer though in tight bends this can be neutralized by pressing the accelerator. The cornering power is very high and the car's line through a corner is virtually impervious to bumps or potholes, even when as occasionally happens on very severe surfaces, the suspension meets its bump stops. The brakes, too, are exceptionally powerful and reassuring. After the car had been put right, there was no more than a trace of the kickback and the stickiness in the steering which contributed to our initial disappointment. In Round Three, then, we judge again the GTB to be the equal of the 246.

Given a little suspension development plus a set of wide, low-profile tyres of the Pirelli P7 kind, it could be even better and perhaps the equal of the latest Porsches.

For comfort the GTB is a clear winner over both the existing 2 + 2 model and the old 246. There's nothing special about its seats which are reasonably comfortable and well shaped, but as in previous Dinos a little short in the backrest and a trifle lacking in lumbar support as well as the lateral support so necessary in a car capable of such high cornering speeds. The driving position, too, remains slightly Italianate; that is, designed for people with long arms and short legs, although this is partly due to the long travel of the clutch pedal which requires the seat to be

depressed position. Ferrari use helper springs to reduce clutch effort, and it is evidently these which become a little officious in their action. Even so, we still rate Round Two as a draw.

So far we have seen that the 308 GTB has two of the characteristics we would demand of a truly great sports car: a magnificent engine and a splendid gearbox. But what about that really essential prerequisite, that *sine qua non*, the handling and road-holding?

At first we were bitterly disappointed: the car understeered strongly, was unstable under heavy braking, floated and bottomed through lack of damping and was put off line on bumps in consequence. But the UK Ferrari importers, Maranello Concessionaires, listened to our complaints, checked the car over and returned it to us with new front dampers, adjusted rear ones and correctly set steering geometry.

The overall effect of this adjustment and maintenance was to transform the car for the

moved closer to the wheel than would otherwise be necessary. And as before there are no separate fresh-air vents.

However, it is possible to obtain, with the help of the fan, a good flow of air – a great improvement on the miserable hot trickle which is all you'd get in a 246. Much more to the point, though, our test car was fitted with the excellent optional air conditioning which kept its interior pleasantly cool during the seemingly almost permanent hot weather.

Another important virtue is the comfort of the ride. There is some harshness when travelling slowly over bumpy surfaces, but at high speeds the movements of the body, always firm and well controlled, smooth out better than in many saloons. These two improvements – to the ventilation and to the ride – coupled with the availability of air conditioning together make the 308 GTB altogether more civilised than the 246.

In our view, however, the car cannot be awarded quite such a high score for refinement. We have nothing but praise for the almost complete absence of wind noise, maintained at the very highest of speeds, nor do we object strongly to the fair amount of bump-thump and road-roar. We are prepared to regard this as being an acceptable price to pay for the car's taut and responsive behaviour, even though we are not wholly convinced that good road noise suppression is incompatible with precision handling. But we do feel that to reduce fatigue on long journeys, the engine could be a little quieter, without losing any of its Ferrari character. Nevertheless the 308 is still quieter than both the 246 and the 2+2.

Despite an overall height no greater than 44.1 in, the Dino has a spacious, airy cockpit providing adequate headroom for tall drivers. There is only enough space behind the seats for a coat or slim briefcase, but plenty of room for luggage in the rear boot with accommodation for a little more in the front boot, above the battery and the narrow-rimmed spare wheel. Under the lids of both these luggage areas are neat zip-up tonneau-type covers.

It is not possible to see the extremities of the long, tapering nose, but the cut-off tail is clearly visible and the all-round view is otherwise good. The main instrument binnacle is also well placed, but its vertical glasses create bad reflections which make the dials difficult to read in daylight. Moreover, the clock and oil temperature gauge are mounted almost out of sight, at the extreme right-hand side of the car under an armrest which, like its twin on the other door, has no purpose other to satisfy some stylist's whim by completing the sweep of the facia.

But if this is a fault of the interior styling, there can be few complaints about the magnificent exterior styling, created by Pininfarina. With a cleaner, crisper shape

than the old 246, the GTB emphasises the essentially nondescript appearance of the 2+2. And the glassfibre panels from which this shape is formed are of exceptional quality, almost wholly lacking in the ripples difficult to eliminate from that material. The same high standard of finish is evident in nearly every other part of the car.

Thus if reincarnation be defined as rebirth on a higher plane, the Ferrari 308 GTB can unhesitatingly be regarded as a worthy descendant of the 246 Dino. It needs some modern ultra low profile tyres, though, to raise its already high cornering powers to the best attainable today.

Not long after this 1975 test of the 308 GTB, Ferrari reverted to metal for all but a few of the exterior panels, and in 1977 added a Targa-topped version to the range, known as the 308 GTS.

GENERAL SPECIFICATION

Engine

Cylinders	8 in vee
Capacity	2927 cc
Bore/stroke	81 × 71 mm
Cooling	water
Block	alloy
Head	alloy
Valves	dohc per bank
Compression	8.8:1
Carburettor	4 Weber 40DCNF twin-choke
Bearings	5 main
Max power	255 (DIN) at 7700 rpm
Max torque	209.8 lb-ft (DIN) at 5000 rpm

Transmission

Type	5-speed manual
Internal ratios and mph/1000 rpm	
Top	0.918:1/21.9
4th	1.244:1/16.1
3rd	1.693:1/11.8
2nd	2.353:1/8.5
1st	3.418:1/5.8
Rev	3.247:1
Final drive	3.71:1

Body/Chassis

Construction	tubular steel chassis with glassfibre panels

Suspension

Front	independent with wishbones, coil springs, anti-roll bar
Rear	independent with wishbones, coil springs, anti-roll bar

Steering

Type	rack and pinion
Assistance	no

Brakes

Front	ventilated discs
Rear	ventilated discs
Servo	yes
Circuit	split front/rear

Wheels/Tyres

Type	alloy, 6½ × 14 in
Tyres	Michelin 205/70 VR14

Electrical

Battery	12v. 60 a-h
Earth	negative
Generator	55 amp alternator
Fuses	18
Headlights	2 halogen

PERFORMANCE DATA

Maximum speeds

	mph	rpm
Top (see text)	150+	—
4th	124	7700
3rd	91	7700
2nd	65	7700
1st	45	7700

Acceleration from rest

mph	sec
0-30	2.8
0-40	3.6
0-50	5.3
0-60	6.8
0-70	8.8
0-80	10.8
0-90	13.7
0-100	16.5
0-110	20.3
0-120	26.2
Standing ¼ mile	14.5
Standing km	26.5

Acceleration

mph	top sec	4th sec
10-30	—	—
20-40	10.7	6.3
30-50	9.7	5.1
40-60	7.7	4.7
50-70	7.2	4.6
60-80	7.1	4.6
70-90	7.1	4.8
80-100	7.8	5.4
90-110	—	6.6
100-120	—	—

Fuel consumption

Touring (estimated)*	19 mpg
Overall (estimated)	14 mpg
Tank capacity	17.6 gal
Max range	334 miles

*Consumption midway between 30 mph and maximum speed less 5% allowance for acceleration.
Maximum range is based on touring consumption.

LOTUS Esprit

With the introduction of the mid-engined Esprit at the end of 1975, Lotus completed the establishment of their new model range, and with it their transformation into manufacturers of high-performance luxury cars in the Ferrari/Porsche mould.

Like its Eclat and Elite stablemates, the Esprit is much more expensive than its respective predecessor, the Lotus Europa. It has a glassfibre body based on a styling exercise by Giugiaro that was exhibited at the 1972 Turin Show – possibly the reason why the Esprit suffers from considerable visibility problems.

A steel backbone chassis is used, with the same water-cooled 16-valve dohc engine of 1973 cc capacity as found in all three current Lotus road cars. With twin 45 DHLA Dellorto carburettors and a 9·5:1 compression ratio, it produces a healthy 160 bhp.

Although the gearbox of the Esprit has five ratios, it bears no resemblance to the Maxi-based unit found in the other Lotus cars, but is supplied by Citroen, for whose now-defunct SM it was developed by Maserati. It also uses the SM linkage.

The Esprit has double-wishbone front suspension, but unlike the other Lotuses, the hubs and links are taken from the Opel Ascona. The rear suspension, in which the driveshafts double as upper links, is traditional Lotus. Braking is by discs all round, mounted inboard at the rear.

At the time of our test the Esprit was significantly cheaper than other contemporary competitors such as the Porsche 911N, Ferrari 308 GTB, Maserati Merak and Lamborghini Uracco – supercars the Esprit matches in some respects, not in others.

It is too wide to swoop through traffic with the same cheekiness as the Europa, and lacks its predecessor's steering sensitivity. On the other hand, its ultimate adhesion limits are so high that few owners are likely to find them, let alone get themselves into difficulties; if they do, they will find the handling very forgiving even on damp surfaces. It is mainly in the areas of noise suppression and visibility – plus a few other niggling faults – that the car disappoints. Development is needed in these areas but even so it deserves to be a success, for it is something of a trend-setter in sports car design.

The twin-cam, belt-driven Lotus engine is very efficient, for from its capacity of 1973 cc no less than 160 bhp is extracted at 6 200 rpm, and it produces 140 lb-ft of torque at 4 900 rpm. This represents more than 81 bhp/litre which is a great deal more than most of its rivals can claim.

The Esprit we tested was not hampered by such encumbrances as air conditioning and the steering is not assisted, so with a lower weight and less power 'leaks', one would expect an appreciable improvement in performance over the other Lotuses. Indeed there is, although we could not approach the claimed figures of 0-60 mph in 6·8 sec or the standing quarter in 15·0 sec, which would really put the Esprit into the supercar class.

However, the times of 7·5 sec to 60 mph and 20·7 sec to 100 mph we got are still excellent. Up to 110 mph it feels quick, but thereafter the acceleration begins to tail off. We just managed to pull 120 mph within the confines of MIRA's acceleration straight.

The Esprit is little slower on acceleration

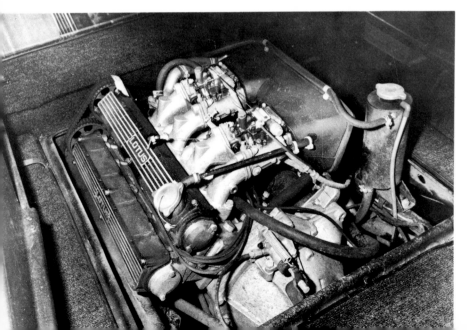

than many more expensive rivals partly because of its superb ability to get off the line so smartly. The traction is astounding – even when the clutch is engaged violently at high engine revs, the Esprit rockets forward leaving only short black lines on the road thanks to its limited slip differential which is a standard fitment.

Lotus claim a maximum speed of 138 mph, which we had no opportunity to verify. However, at 125 mph it had something in hand so over 130 mph is probably feasible.

Mid-range acceleration is very brisk, all the increments between 50 mph and 90 mph in fourth gear taking between 7·2 sec and 7·6 sec; this is the vital range for overtaking and the Esprit performs very well in it. Bearing in mind that top is intended purely for cruising, acceleration in this gear is not bad either.

Lotus have made a great play about the economy of their range. We achieved 20·3 mpg in the course of our test, quite good for a high performance two-litre car. Restrained driving could give over 25 mpg although we doubt if anyone would approach what Lotus describe as an 'overall touring' figure of 33 mpg. A reasonable range of 373 miles is obtainable from the 14·8 gallons contained in twin tanks.

Gear linkage design is frequently the worst feature of cars whose engines are situated behind the driver. However, excellence with this configuration is by no means unattainable, as Porsche so ably demonstrate. The gearchange of the Esprit is even better – lighter to move and less notchy – and an improvement over that of the last Europa.

The gate is narrow with a short throw and the pattern is conventional, with fifth set over to the right, and reverse below it. Accidental selection of the latter is prevented by the necessity to lift the lever over an obstruction.

Fifth gear is described on the lever as 'Overdrive', an apt description of its nature although technically incorrect. At relatively high speeds in top, up to about 90 mph, the Esprit is quite economical and reasonably quiet. The other ratios are equally well suited to the characteristics and purpose of the car, being nicely spaced with maxima of 40, 61, 89 and 121 mph. The engine will not pull from below 40 mph in top, but it is much more flexible in fourth. The clutch is light and smooth.

The traction is almost beyond compare in a road car, even better than that of a Porsche, especially in the wet. The fat tyres are 205s all round, but they are 70-series at the rear and 60-series at the front on 7J and 6J rims respectively, instead of the differing tyre widths used in early versions. The limit of adhesion on dry surfaces is astonishing and even on wet roads it is very impressive.

The Esprit is an exceptionally safe car, although perhaps not so much fun to drive as the Elan Sprint. It does not respond to an

extrovert tail-out driving style – indeed such an attitude is very hard to achieve; an increase in power merely increases the understeer, while lifting off in mid-corner provokes a mild tightening of the line.

Unlike the front-engined cars, the Esprit is not offered with power-assisted steering. Its rack and pinion system is nicely weighted but does not have quite the same precision as that of its forebears. It is a bit lifeless until lock is applied, and even then there is not quite the sensitivity and feel we had expected. On the other hand the car is astonishingly stable and runs arrow straight at very high speeds, the bib spoiler holding the front end down well except in strong cross winds.

Large discs – inboard at the back – are fitted all round. The excellent servo has not impaired the sensitivity of the braking, which is stable and reassuring. Relatively low pedal pressures achieve 1·0 g stops, and despite the fact that the pads began to smell, no fade showed up in testing.

The Esprit is designed to carry two adults and their luggage, and it fulfils this function better than most mid-engined cars. For tall and bulky people, getting in and out is rather awkward despite the wide doors, and in bad weather the cloth-covered sill over which you must slide gets wet and dirty; it's also likely that your shoes will scuff the seat on the way in.

The huge rear door is hinged at the door pillar line and supported by a pair of struts. It gapes to allow easy loading over a low ledge, but the carpet of our test car was soaked with rain, causing severe internal condensation. The luggage area is generous for this type of vehicle, and a tonneau is supplied to shield valuables from the gaze of potential miscreants. A small amount of extra luggage may be stored in the nose section, which is mostly taken up by the spare wheel. Apart from the unlockable glove box and a small cubbyhole on the central armrest there is scarcely any stowage space in the passenger compartment, although flat objects may be squeezed behind the seats.

will find the left-hand switches too far away. The left-hand stalk operates the two-speed wiper and the windscreen washer, and the indicators, flasher, main beam and horn are operated by the other. The choke lever and the electric window lifters are handily placed on the central console, behind the gearlever.

Lotus have no doubt applied much thought to the problem of visibility out of the Esprit, but a great deal more will be required if they are to solve it, for it has many of the worst faults associated with a mid-engined car, plus a couple more caused by reflections in the division window and the rear side panes.

Forward visibility is awkward for parking unless the headlights are raised, although it is quite good otherwise, marred only slightly by thick pillars and light reflection. It is essential at all times to remember that not only is this a very wide car, but also that its widest point, over the rear wheels, is out of sight. Fortunately, a plastic scuff strip along the waistline protects the paintwork from minor scrapes.

The view out of the rear screen is acceptable once the car is on the move, but rearward and rear three-quarter vision is very poor indeed for reversing or manoeuvring in tight spaces. Emergence from angled side turnings demands a van driver's technique. An additional problem we encountered was misting-up of the rear side windows, which do not contain a heating element and cannot be reached from the passenger compartment. Even the heater for the back window failed to cope with condensation from the wet boot carpets.

The single two-speed wiper has a broad sweep and the flat glass aids its efficiency, but a small area to the right adds to the blind spot caused by the thick pillar on right-hand bends. The electrically lifted twin headlights have a good range on both dipped and main beams, but they suffer from vibration over bumps which makes them flicker.

The Esprit's Veglia instruments are attractively styled with green backgrounds and quite well calibrated. Two major dials – the speedometer and rev-counter – dominate the console, with an oil pressure gauge and water temperature gauge to the left and the fuel gauge and a battery condition indicator to the right, all these four instruments being semi-circular. There is a display of warning lights running along the top of the console.

The heating controls, grouped on the right of the console, are clearly marked and easy to understand, although invisible in the dark. There are two levers which move in the horizontal plane, one for distribution and the other for temperature control which is progressive in its action. Even with the two-speed fan full on the output of hot air is not enormous, although once warmed up the heater copes well enough.

Drivers of average size will almost certainly find the interior of the Esprit very much to their liking. The stylish lightweight seats with their practical built-in headrests are nearly as comfortable as they look, and there is sufficient fore/aft adjustment in the runners. However, the backrests – which do not give enough side support – are fixed so you are forced to adopt a semi-reclining position which not everyone liked.

Apart from restricted headroom, the larger driver may be put off by the interference of his knee with the comparatively large, non-adjustable steering wheel when operating the clutch; similarly, anyone with big feet will find the pendant pedals too close together. Nor is there much space between the clutch pedal and the central tunnel; a left-foot rest would be welcome. Moreover, there is a danger of depressing the throttle linkage crossbar while resting your left foot.

The relationship between the major controls is generally good, except for the handbrake, which is too far forward on the right.

Most of the minor controls are set into the neat instrument pod and they are all within easy reach of most drivers although some

Although directional control of the two face-level fresh air vents is admirable, there is little throughput. Exhaust gases wafted into the car in traffic take a long time to waft out again, and usually it is advisable to open a window in such circumstances.

In this price class one would expect peace and quiet and that any intruding noise would at least be a nice noise: the Esprit is disappointing in this respect. The engine cover does little to banish the loud boom that is particularly obtrusive beyond 4000 rpm. Even so, as fifth is so high, the engine remains fairly quiet when cruising at 90 mph. The transmission is relatively quiet.

Wind roar, poorly suppressed at speed, comes mainly around the door pillars. There's also quite a lot of bump-thump over really rough surfaces although on the whole road noise is quite subdued despite the size of the tyres.

The Esprit's ride comfort is generally impressive, for major road surface irregularities are ironed our smoothly; only the occasional deep rut causes jarring. Once again Lotus have proved (if proof were needed) that it is not essential to sacrifice a civilised ride in pursuit of taut handling, or indeed vice versa. Roll is virtually absent, there is no appreciable float, and hardly any pitch or squat even under severe braking and acceleration.

The Esprit's specification includes electric windows, a laminated screen, heated rear window, door mirror, hazard warning lights, inertia-reel seat belts and a two-stage panel light. What it does not include is a clock, rear window wiper and a cigarette lighter, all extraordinary omissions.

The attractive Wolfrace wheels are not, as may be seen from the pictures, matched front to rear. The spare is a front wheel and tyre so in the event of a puncture at the back caution must be observed. A small toolkit is supplied as well as the jack and wheelbrace.

The interior of the Esprit is plush and modern. Our test car was trimmed in brown suede-like fabric, colour coded to the cream brushed nylon of the seats. The carpet's beige shade fell somewhere between these two. Surprisingly, the carpet in the boot is grey. There is an alternative of tartan and green cloth.

Despite one or two creaks and rattles in our test car, the Esprit is fitted out quite well, although we would like to see scuff-plates on the doors. We were not impressed by the flimsy sun visors or hinges of the glove box, while the positioning and size of the ashtrays renders them virtually useless.

The external finish is excellent, showing just how much Lotus have advanced in recent years.

Lotus unveiled a Series 2 Esprit in late 1978, which *Motor* tested in early 1979. The engine proved more flexible than its predecessor's, but remained noisy and boomy, while other failings of poor visibility and meagre ventilation remained substantially unchanged. Minor suspension and steering revisions have, however, effected an improvement in steering feel.

SPECIFICATION

Engine

Cylinders	4 in line, mid-mounted
Capacity	1973 cc
Bore/stroke	95·2 × 62·9 mm
Cooling	water
Block	aluminium
Head	aluminium
Valves	dohc
Compression	9·5:1
Carburettor	2 Dellorto DHLA45E
Bearings	5 main
Max power	160 bhp (DIN) at 6200 rpm
Max torque	140 lb-ft (DIN) at 4900 rpm

Transmission

Type	5-speed manual
Internal ratios and mph/1000 rpm	
Top	0·760:1/22·1
4th	0·970:1/17·3
3rd	1·320:1/12·7
2nd	1·940:1/8·7
1st	2·920:1/5·8
Rev	3·460:1
Final drive	4·375:1

Body/Chassis

Construction	steel backbone chassis with glassfibre body

Suspension

Front	independent by unequal length wishbones, coil springs, anti-roll bar
Rear	independent by lower transverse links, fixed length driveshafts, semi-trailing arms and coil springs

Steering

Type	rack and pinion
Assistance	no

Brakes

Front	discs
Rear	inboard discs
Servo	yes
Circuit	split, front/rear

Wheels/Tyres

Type	alloy, 6J × 14 in (front), 7J × 14 in (rear)
Tyres	205/60 HR14 (front); 205/70 HR14 (rear)

Electrical

Battery	12v, 44 a-h
Earth	negative
Generator	alternator
Fuses	4
Headlights	4 × 75/60W

PERFORMANCE DATA

Maximum speeds

		mph	rpm
Top (see text)	...	130+	—
4th	...	121	7000
3rd	...	89	7000
2nd	...	61	7000
1st	...	40	7000

Acceleration from rest

mph					sec
0-30	...				2·5
0-40	...				3·8
0-50	...				5·4
0-60	...				7·5
0-70	...				9·9
0-80	...				12·8
0-90	...				16·2
0-100	...				20·7
0-110	...				27·8
0-120	...				40·0
Standing ¼ mile					16·1
Standing km			...		29·6

Acceleration in

mph			top	4th
			sec	sec
40-60	...	...	12·4	8·1
50-70	...	...	12·7	7·4
60-80	...	...	11·9	7·2
70-90	...	...	11·8	7·6
80-100	...	...	13·5	8·6
90-110	...	...	—	12·2

Fuel consumption

Touring*	25·2 mpg
Overall	20·3 mpg
Tank capacity	14·8 gal
Max range	373 miles

*Consumption midway between 30 mph and maximum speed, less 5% allowance for acceleration.
Maximum range is based on touring consumption.

ASTON MARTIN
Vantage V8

Britain came perilously close to losing a vital part of her motoring heritage in June 1974 as, but for the Eleventh Hour intervention of American and Canadian interests, Aston Martin and Lagonda would have faded into history. Since then our New World cousins have rekindled the spirit that won Aston Martin their coveted Le Mans victory and are accelerating the rejuvenated firm back to the fore of the automotive world.

What the company needed more than most was a new model, a prestige carriage to tap the interest and custom of the rich. Realising this a new generation Lagonda appeared

almost overnight to steal the 1976 London Motor Show. In the shadow cast by the star studded attraction stood the model with which the company's fortunes had oscillated since October 1967: the Aston Martin V8 (nee DBS).

Dismissed as anachronistic by the uninitiated and almost unknown to many, the V8 is worshipped by those lucky enough to have driven one. Perhaps it does not bear the sharp aggressive lines of the futuristic looking Lamborghini Countach, or the relatively light, efficient frame of a Lotus Elite. But it does possess outstanding performance, and

extraordinarily high levels of handling and adhesion which it combines with the traditional craftsmanship for which British cars were once renowned and after which many still hanker. Such comments are never more valid than when applied to the V8 Vantage, the most electrifying version of the Aston Martin V8 yet.

The Vantage has considerably more power than even the standard car although as Aston never quote power figures, we are reduced to making an educated guess. Uprated camshafts, larger inlet valves and carburettors and special inlet manifolds must have raised the output by around 40 per cent however – meaning phenomenal power by any standards. Supporting the theory is the fact that when committed to the rigours of standing start accelerations AM V8 – said to be 37 bhp down on power – still returned almost identical figures to our old pre-emission car of 1973!

Feeding the clutch in sharply with the engine howling in excess of 5000 rpm the Aston stormed off the line leaving a weaving trail of spent rubber in its wake. It takes bags of power and not a little adhesion to do that. The car reached 30 mph in a mere 2·2 sec and in fact the number of current production cars that will scorch to 60 mph in under 6 sec can be counted on one hand. What is more the experience is the type that sets your nerves tingling however often you do it.

Yet, so disappointed were Aston Martin and *Motor* with the results achieved with an engine 37 bhp down on power that we made a second attempt – after Aston had diagnosed and cured an excess of back-pressure in the exhaust system – to substantiate their claim that the Vantage V8 is the fastest production car in the world.

During our first test we had dropped the clutch at 5000 rpm for the best results; this time we found 3000 rpm was nearer the mark. Even then we left black lines too long to pace out. We had the okay to use considerably more revs through the gears, too; in other words to pull well into the red line.

This time traction was definitely the problem and to 50 mph at least the times (shown in brackets in the data panel) were worse than before. From there on, however, the tremendous power of the Aston's home-grown all-alloy V8 was being transmitted to the tarmac in no uncertain terms. Where the Aston loses out, as does the Ferrari Boxer, is with its dog-leg first-to-second gearchange. Snappy though the ZF gearbox is, that awkward movement definitely loses valuable fractions of a second.

We persevered, gradually reducing the take-off revs and finding fractionally more grip. The 0-120 mph times were coming down, now 1½ seconds better than before, then bang. An unprecedented failure in the output shaft of the Salisbury differential brought our bid for yet better times to a dramatic and unplanned halt.

What a pity. Our reunion with Newport Pagnell's ultimate offering had heightened our enthusiasm for the traditional way of doing things. Sure, mid-engined cars have a special place on the race track but there is that little undefinable something about powerful, front-engined rear-drive cars on the road; especially when they possess the feel and predictability of the Aston. The manufacturers claimed it to be the fastest production car in the world, but we have yet to verify the claim. Our impression, though, is that no Ferrari could beat it.

Helped by the sheer precision of the superb ZF gearbox, the Aston's acceleration is relentless. There is only a hint of a pause between changes before you are pressed firmly back in the seat once more. Before braking for the ends of MIRA's one mile straights the car was pulling close on 140 mph.

Its ultimate speed? Well, it will pull its red line of 148 mph with disdain and has more than enough power to cap its predecessor's best of 154·8 mph, despite its special low final drive ratio. To match Aston's claim of 167 mph it would be pulling nearly 6800 rpm, a figure we have no reason to doubt.

Just as impressive as the flat out acceleration is the uncanny pull in top gear. At a mere 1000 rpm in fifth the throttle can be floored, opening wide all eight chokes of the fat Weber carburettors. So instantaneous is the response that cog-swapping is often needless even around town. Even in its high state of tune the Aston's British-built V8 is totally untemperamental. It bursts into life with just a few pumps of the throttle whatever the ambient temperature, and when warm settles at an unfussed 900 rpm.

One of many minor changes that comprise the Vantage package is the raising of the fuel capacity from 21 to 30 gallons (an option on the standard car), a very necessary tweak when you realise that Aston's new road burner averaged exactly 10·0 mpg. Obviously we made full use of the available acceleration but were never able to cruise at sustained high speed. It seems reasonable to assume that fast trans-continental runs would have brought the figure even lower! However, we strongly suspect that the problems that caused the loss of performance also affected the consumption – 13-14 mpg being a more likely average.

We could find nothing but praise for the handling of our last V8 test car and if anything the behaviour of the Vantage was even more satisfying. Happily Aston Martin have done their uprating thoroughly and with the extra power come suspension and brakes to suit. Rubber has been used to give progressive springing at the rear and the diameter of the front anti-roll bar has been increased. Koni telescopic dampers are now standard all round. Even wider section tyres on the standard 7 in alloy rims ensure further adhesion and a deep air dam for the front and boot lid spoiler for the rear are aimed at reducing lift and giving superior high-speed stability. The net result of these changes is a car that evoked fresh enthusiasm for driving on our over-crowded roads.

The Adwest power steering – full of feel on and off lock – combined with the predictability of the well sorted chassis, gives the effect of a car half the Aston's size and weight; a car that can be driven hard and with confidence. So adhesive are the fat, 60 series Pirelli tyres that most drivers will rarely find themselves in true poses of understeer or oversteer. Suffice to say that if pushed to the limit in the dry or wet the weighty nose will cling on grimly, as will the rear, until deliberately provoked by the tremendous power. Only in torrential rain does the considerable width of the high-grip tyres call for respect, lest they aquaplane.

Huge ventilated disc brakes, slotted and set outboard at the front, inboard at the rear, wrench the Aston down from speed without any hint of strain, glazing, noise or fade. The pedal is heavy, even a mite dead in feel, but the power of the dual circuit system is never in doubt.

Outwardly the Vantage is recognisable by its deep bib spoiler, the blanked-off intake and radiator grille with its inset lights and the boot-lid spoiler. Some thought the aids detracted from the gracious lines of the original William Towns design, others felt they just endowed the car with an even more masculine, purposeful air.

Inside there is little or nothing to give the game away. The seats are the same hide-covered recliners we enjoyed in the last car, and even the bank of instruments and bevy of switches all looked familiar. Time has changed and improved some items, however. The clutch was notably lighter than before, and the ZF gearbox no longer baulked, proving sheer joy to use despite its old-fashioned dog-leg first to second change. The organ throttle pedal has been changed for a pendant type while the others still sprout from the floor.

Despite the auxiliary driving lamps the total light power seemed insufficient for a car of such extreme performance – perhaps they needed re-setting. Other lights exist in abundance, however, with courtesy operated ones for the interior, bonnet and boot, automatic ones for reversing and a swivel one for map reading. Other nice touches include the traditional fly-off handbrake, the town/country horn, the battery master switch, the telescopic steering column and the pair of fillers for the vast petrol tank.

Had that elusive 37 bhp been on tap at the time of our test the figures would more than have justified the Vantage's extra cost over the everyman's V8. As it was the car completely re-awakened our almost unbounded enthusiasm for cars of that ilk. Far from being just a show-piece the Vantage is a true thoroughbred that combines the very best in performance and road manners with quality of workmanship.

Maybe it is both heavy and thirsty by modern standards, but it has more than enough power to overcome its bulk and has that feeling of longevity and well-being that is lacking in many rival Supercars.

Exciting though their space-age Lagonda is, we hope Aston Martin continue to unleash their V8s on the world for many years yet. Speed restrictions or no, life wouldn't be quite the same without them.

There was no major changes to the Aston Martin Vantage subsequently to our test; in 1978 it gained an improved interior finish, in common with the other versions, and was joined by the exclusive Volante convertible variation on the "standard" V8 saloon.

GENERAL SPECIFICATION

Engine

Cylinders	8 in vee
Capacity	5340 cc
Bore/stroke	100 × 85 mm
Cooling	water
Block	alloy
Head	alloy
Valves	dohc
Compression	9:1
Carburettor	4 Weber twin-choke
Bearings	5 main
Max power	not quoted
Max torque	not quoted

Transmission

Type	5-speed ZF manual

Internal ratios and mph/1000 rpm

Top	0·845:1	24·7
4th	1·000:1	20·9
3rd	1·220:1	17·1
2nd	1·780:1	11·7
1st	2·900:1	7·2
Rev	2·630:1	
Final drive	3·77:1	

Body/Chassis

Construction	steel platform chassis, steel superstructure, aluminium panels

Suspension

Front	independent by wishbones, coil springs, anti-roll bar
Rear	independent by de Dion axle located by parallel links, Watts linkage, coil springs

Steering

Type	Adwest rack and pinion
Assistance	yes

Brakes

Front	ventilated discs
Rear	ventilated discs
Servo	yes
Circuit	dual

Wheels/Tyres

Type	alloy, 7 × 15 in
Tyres	Pirelli 255/60 VR15

Electrical

Battery	12v, 68 a-h
Earth	negative
Generator	alternator
Fuses	12
Headlights	2 halogen, plus auxiliary driving lights

PERFORMANCE DATA

Maximum speeds

	mph	rpm
Top (see text) ...	167	6800
4th	125	6000
3rd	103	6000
2nd	70	6000
1st	43	6000

Acceleration from rest

mph				sec	
0-30 ...	...	...		2·2	(2·6)
0-40 ...		...		3·1	(3·4)
0-50 ...			...	4·4	(4·7)
0-60 ...				5·8	(5·8)
0-70 ...				7·2	(7·3)
0-80 ...				9·1	(8·9)
0-90 ...				11·1	(10·7)
0-100...				13·6	(12·9)
0-110...				17·0	(16·0)
0-120...				20·7	(19·4)
Standing ¼ mile		...		14·0	
Standing km..		...		25·2	

Acceleration in

mph		top sec		4th sec
10-30	...	—	—	—
20-40	...	—	—	—
30-50	...	—		5·8
40-60	...	6·9	(6·0)	5·3
50-70	...	6·8	(5·5)	5·1
60-80	...	6·6	(5·7)	4·8
70-90	...	6·4	(5·7)	5·2
80-100	...	6·4	(5·8)	5·0
90-110	...	7·2	—	5·9
100-120	...	8·2	—	7·2

Fuel consumption

Touring (estimated)*	14 mpg
Overall	10 mpg
Tank capacity	30 gal
Maximum range	420 miles

*Consumption midway between 30 mph and maximum speed less 5% allowance for acceleration. Maximum range is based on touring consumption.

PORSCHE 928

How to follow up on a legend, was Porsche's dilemma when it decided to add a larger, more luxurious and dearer car to its range up-market of the charismatic 911.

As a manufacturer producing only sports cars, Porsche knew its new car would have to live up to an almost unrivalled sporting reputation; but as a manufacturer dependent on the sports car, Porsche would also have to safeguard its future with a car compatible with political and ecological climates ever more hostile to the idea of the sports car as a temperamental, anti-social plaything for the selfish hedonist.

Porsche's solution was the 928, a striking 2+2 coupe revealed to an awestruck world in 1977 and subsequently winner of the 1978 Car of the Year award. Technically, it was no surprise that the 911's fundamentally unsound rear engine layout was discarded, but more surprising is the rejection of the theoretically supreme – in sporting terms – mid engine layout. Instead, for the sakes of space and practicality, it has a conventional front engine/rear wheel drive layout, although it is less conventional in detail with the five-speed gearbox mounted at the rear in unit with the final drive.

The water-cooled all-alloy V8 has a capacity of 4474 cc. Fuel is supplied by Bosch K-Jetronic injection through in-line valves actuated by a single overhead cam on each bank. With a compression ratio of 8·5:1, the engine produces 240 bhp (DIN) at 5500 rpm; a respectable enough output, but with hydraulic tappets and using 91 octane fuel it also reflects the overall emphasis on durability and low maintenance costs before the ultimate in performance.

Perhaps the fact that the 928 was not even the dearest Porsche is a clue to why it did not entirely live up to our expectations, for impressive though the performance and handling are, they do not set new standards, while overall refinement is let down by excessive road noise. In the final analysis, while the 928 undoubtedly is a most desirable car even by the exacting standards of its class, it is not after all The Ultimate.

But if the 928 does not raise Porsche performance standards on to an even higher plane, it does introduce a new docility and effortlessness as exemplified by 257 lb-ft of torque peaking at 3600 rpm and the ability to accelerate sweetly and sturdily from below 500 rpm in fourth gear. Adequate performance, with (almost) unmatched civility, seems to be the message.

For the truth is that by Supercar standards the 928's outright performance is unexceptional. To accelerate from 0-60 mph in 7·0 sec and to 100 mph in 17·8 sec makes the 928 no sluggard, but the Jaguar, the Aston Martin and the Ferrari do it faster. In top gear, too, the 928 sets no new standards.

We were unable to record a true maximum speed in the 928, but the speeds we *were* able to reach suggest that 140 mph is about it, all out, even though Porsche claims 143 mph.

But, to coin a cliché, it's not what the car does, but the way it does it. So quiet is the Porsche's V8 engine, and so smooth (apart from a slight throbby vibration over 4000 rpm) that what performance it has can be more fully exploited than in many of its rivals, although the XJS, for one, is even better. It feels able to maintain maximum speed all day in its loping fifth gear, or for

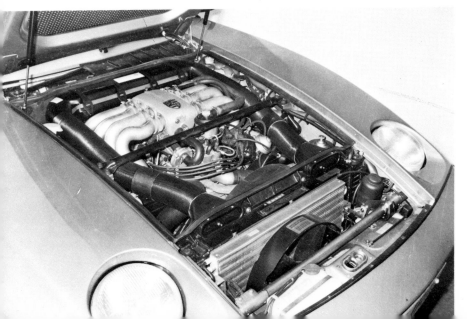

vivid overtaking acceleration (30-50 mph in 5·4 sec, 50-70 mph in 5·2 sec and 70-90 mph in 5·6 sec) you can stay in fourth all day on give and take roads without a hint of strain from the engine. Or you can simply trickle along in traffic with fewer than 1000 rpm on the clock and know that when your chance comes to open up again, the engine will respond without a hint of hesitation or temperament.

By Supercar standards the 928's overall fuel consumption of 14·9 mpg is reasonably thrifty, although by Porsche's own standards – in comparison to what past 911 test cars have achieved – it is nothing special. It should be borne in mind, though, that unlike most of its rivals, the 928 only requires the cheapest grade of fuel.

In virtually every aspect of its design the 928's transmission is unconventional, from the gate pattern of its gearchange, through the twin-plate clutch and torque-tube-enclosed propeller shaft, to the mounting of its five-speed gearbox in unit with the final drive at the rear axle.

The gate pattern places the top four forward gears in a conventional H pattern, with first over to the left and back (with reverse opposite) and so requiring a dog-leg movement for the first-to-second change. The resulting gearchange does take some getting used to: there is a strong spring loading from the 1st/reverse plane to the 2nd/3rd plane, and you must learn to leave it to the spring loading to find the 2nd gear slot when changing up – if you consciously try to guide the lever across the gate you may well end up in 4th instead. On the other hand, the lack of spring loading between 2nd/3rd and 4th/5th does require some conscious guidance from the driver when changing up and (especially) when changing down.

Once the change is learned, however, it proves fast and light, although the powerful synchromesh means that downchanges are considerably eased by double declutching. The clutch has an unusually long travel – which must be used to its full extent for clean gearchanges – and is light to operate, although prone to judder if you try to pull away with too few revs.

Spacing of the gearbox ratios is generally very good, with a very long-legged fifth giving 26·5 mph per 1000 rpm, although fourth could usefully be made a little taller and so closer to fifth.

The 928 has power-assisted rack and pinion steering that is among the best available on any car – you are rarely aware that there is any assistance. Direct, very precise and nicely weighted, the only possible criticism of the steering is a degree of lifelessness about the straightahead position compared with that of, say, an Aston Martin – it improves on lock and does provide real 'feel' of what the front wheels are doing.

Although the steering is not especially high geared, the sheer 'bite' of the low profile tyres ensures sharp response to the helm. So far as most drivers will ever experience it, the 928's handling is of the proverbial 'on rails. variety as the dry road adhesion of the Pirelli P7 tyres is very high. The car can be flicked through tight corners at very high speeds with little of the expected scrubby understeer, tyre squeal or roll.

As speeds rise still further there is a steady increase in safe stable understeer, and although the 928 can be persuaded to over-steer it needs to be deliberately provoked. You can do it by throwing the car into a corner, or by really pouring on the power in a low gear. The Porsche-Weissach rear axle ensures that there is no instant oversteer should you lift off the throttle in mid-bend, but there is a pronounced tuck-in effect which can be used to counter excessive understeer near the limit.

But if and when you do get the tail to step out of line, the breakaway is not always as tidy and progressive as we would like, especially if the road is less than smooth. Similarly, the 928 does not always inspire total confidence at speed on an uneven road, when the wheels tend to follow cambers and you may even experience a tendency to float on humps.

We were generally highly impressed by the 928's stability at speed on a motorway and the way it sits four-square on the road through long bends at desperately illegal speeds, but there are times when it causes some disquiet. If you need to brake hard for a bend at three-figure speeds the 928 feels unstable as it enters the bend – a tendency to float and weave disconcertingly, although once committed to the bend its usual imperturbability is restored.

Large ventilated disc brakes on all four wheels, with floating calipers and servo assistance, add up to a braking specification that is well matched to the 928's weight and speed.

At low speeds the brakes feel rather dead, and need a hefty push for maximum deceleration, but they are nicely progressive, giving a maximum deceleration of 1·0 g plus, for 95 lb pedal pressure. An extra safety bonus is the extreme reluctance of the wheels to lock up and skid even in a panic stop.

Predictably, the Porsche sailed through our fade test (involving 20 successive 0·5 g stops at 1 minute intervals from 90 mph) with ease, the required pressures actually dropping a little towards the end of the test as the brakes warmed to their task.

A good 0·38 g deceleration was achieved using the handbrake only from 30 mph, although a very hefty yank on the handbrake lever was required to hold the car facing down the 1 in 3 hill.

The rear window of the 928 must be the only one in the world to feature its own wash/wipe system, demisting *and* sunvisors

It is usual (although by no means compulsory) among cars of this class to sacrifice some ride comfort – especially at low speeds – in pursuance of taut and sporting handling. The Porsche is no exception to this norm, but in its overall ride/handling compromise the 928 is not as successful as some rivals. It is distinctly firm and restless at low speeds on small bumps, accompanied by a lot of bump thump, and large sharp disturbances can cause quite a sharp jolt.

At speed the ride does improve, but not to the same degree as in some rivals, and we were a little surprised and disappointed to observe a very slight tendency to float at times on humps and bumps, especially when the car was laden with passengers and luggage.

Considered purely as a 2-seater the 928 is extremely spacious, with an enormous amount of legroom in the front and good headroom.

As a four-seater, however, the 928 must be considered strictly as a 2+2. To travel four

up, even with passengers of only average height, entails a degree of compromise on legroom that could only be tolerated for short journeys, while headroom in the rear is very limited.

With the rear seat in use, only 5·3 cu ft of luggage can be accommodated if you want to have the luggage cover in place, although another 2 cu ft can be squeezed if you do not clip the cover right down.

A notable feature of the 928's cockpit is that when you adjust the rake of the steering wheel, the whole steering column and instrument binnacle moves with it, thus maintaining the correct relationship between wheel, switches and instruments.

This feature, in combination with sensible location of major and minor controls, enables most drivers to find a comfortable attitude at the wheel although the very low seating position was commented on even by our tallest testers and the shorter ones found it awkward to see out.

Most of the minor switches are well located, with two column stalks for wash/wipe and indicators/dip/flash respectively. There is a group of three large rotary knobs for driving lights, and front and rear fog lamps, and two similar knobs for the rear wipe and heated rear window.

Even tall drivers found the 928 awkward to see out of, especially for parking, when the drooping nose of the car is invisible and the bulbous sides make it very difficult to judge the car's width. For short drivers the low seating position only aggravates the situation.

In terms of both their quantity and quality it is hard to fault the 928's instruments. There are six beautifully calibrated gauges, well located in a single housing under an angled pane of glass that effectively banishes all reflections, and the instruments are beautifully illuminated at night.

The 928's heating and ventilation controls are fairly straightforward, with a rotary knob for the 5-speed fan, and upper and lower slides governing temperature and distribution respectively.

Over most of its range the temperature slide control gives fine graduation of temperature, except for one point in its travel where the transition from merely warm to hot occurs very abruptly.

The fan is only acceptably quiet at the lowest three of its five speeds, but is capable of an impressive throughput of air.

In addition to its very effective air conditioning unit fitted as standard, the Porsche also has a fairly versatile fresh air ventilation system, with two face-level vents in the centre of the facia which supply air at ambient temperature but with a flow that can be fan boosted, and their own individual volume control. These provide an adequate flow of air provided the fan is used, although

maximum throughput is reduced progressively as the heater temperature is increased: at least it is possible, unlike with many air conditioned cars, to have cool air to the face along with warm to the foot-wells, even if it is not always easy to achieve the right combination of both, so sometimes resulting in a stuffy effect.

When a manufacturer with Porsche's pedigree introduces an all-new luxury sports car with a low-stressed V8 engine, you might expect the level of refinement to be something special. But if considered in these terms, the 928 proves somewhat of a disappointment.

This is certainly not to say that it is a noisy car: the engine is virtually silent at modest speeds and remains refined even at peak revs; in the right conditions it is entirely feasible to cruise at 120 mph or more in complete relaxation.

But in adverse conditions of road surface and wind strength, the 928 shows up rather poorly compared to, say, a Jaguar XJ-S. Even at very modest speeds there is excessive bump thump and, above all, tyre roar on all but the finest surfaces – characteristics which, of course, remain at higher speeds. Indeed, even at the very highest cruising speeds, road noise usually dominates that from engine or wind noise.

The latter can be low on a still day or with a following wind – especially if you keep speeds down to 70 or 80 mph – but may become noticeable at higher speeds in blowy conditions, although never reaching excessive levels.

Not all our testers found the 928's distinctive styling to their taste, but none could deny the immaculate finishing of the curvaceous body panels and the metallic paintwork.

The story is much the same inside the car; the rather loud check pattern of the seats' cloth inserts was disliked by some, but all recognised the nicely integrated interior styling, the tasteful blending of leather and plastic trim panels, the high standard of detail finish.

Even by the elevated standards of its price, the 928 is exceptionally well equipped. The only extra cost option on our test car was the passenger side door mirror;

even the air conditioning and stereo radio/cassette (with four speakers and front/rear balance control) are standard, while other items include electrically adjustable and heated door mirrors, and an excellent cruise control system with re-set facility.

Porsche's 928 has not undergone any significant changes since this test was carried out in October 1978, although a point worth noting is that a height-adjustable front seat is available on most markets which should answer most of our criticisms relating to the low driving position and visibility problems.

The entire instrument display moves up and down in unison with the adjustable steering wheel

GENERAL SPECIFICATION

Engine

Cylinders	8 in vee
Capacity	4 474 cc
Bore/stroke	95 × 78·9 mm
Cooling	water
Block	alloy
Head	alloy
Valves	sohc per bank
Compression	8·5:1
Fuel injection	Bosch K-Jetronic
Bearings	5 main
Max power	240 bhp (DIN) at 5 500 rpm
Max torque	257 lb-ft (DIN) at 3 600 rpm

Transmission

Type	5-speed manual, rear-mounted transaxle

Internal ratios and mph/1000 rpm

Top	1:1	26·5
4th	1·34:1	19·8
3rd	1·75:1	15·2
2nd	2·46:1	10·8
1st	3·60:1	7·4
Rev	3·16:1	
Final drive	2·75:1	

Body/Chassis

Construction	steel monocoque with alloy doors, bonnet and front wings

Suspension

Front	independent by double wishbones, strut type dampers with co-axial coil springs, anti-roll bar
Rear	independent by lower wishbones, upper transverse links (Porsche-Weissach patent geometry), coil springs, telescopic dampers, anti-roll bar

Steering

Type	rack and pinion
Assistance	yes

Brakes

Front	11·1 in ventilated discs
Rear	11·4 in ventilated discs
Servo	yes
Circuit	split diagonally

Wheels/Tyres

Type	alloy, 7J × 16 in
Tyres	Pirelli P7 225/50 VR16

Electrical

Battery	12v, 66 a-h
Earth	negative
Generator	90 amp alternator
Fuses	34
Headlights	2 halogen H4

PERFORMANCE DATA

Maximum speeds		mph	rpm
Top (estimted)	...	140	5 300
4th	... ...	119	6 000
3rd	... ...	91	6 000
2nd	... ...	65	6 000
1st	... ...	44	6 000

Acceleration from rest		
mph		sec
0-30	... ...	2·7
0-40	... ...	3·7
0-50	... ...	5·4
0-60	... ...	7·0
0-70	... ...	9·0
0-80	... ...	11·2
0-90	... ...	14·5
0-100	... ...	17·8
0-110	... ...	22·6
0-120	... ...	31·3
Standing ¼ mile	... ...	15·2
Standing km	... ...	27·7

Acceleration in		top	4th
mph		sec	sec
10-30	... ...	—	6·0
20-40	... ...	8·0	5·6
30-50	... ...	7·8	5·4
40-60	... ...	7·9	5·4
50-70	... ...	7·9	5·2
60-80	... ...	8·4	5·2
70-90	... ...	8·7	5·6
80-100	... ...	9·4	6·4
90-110	... ...	10·9	8·3
100-120	... ...	—	14·0

Fuel consumption	
Touring (estimated)*	18 mpg
Overall	14·9 mpg
Tank capacity	18·9 gal
Max range	340 miles

*Consumption midway between 30 mph and maximum speed less 5% allowance for acceleration.
Maximum range is based on touring consumption.